THE REASON FOR DEMOCRACY

Also by Kalman H. Silvert

Education, Class and Nation

Man's Power: A Biased Guide to Political Thought

The Conflict Society: Reaction and Revolution in Latin America

Chile Yesterday and Today

A Study in Government: Guatemala

Edited by Kalman H. Silvert

The Social Reality of Scientific Myth

Expectant Peoples: Nationalism and Development

Churches and States: The Religious Institution and Modernization

Discussion at Bellagio: The Political Alternatives of Development

THE
REASON
FOR
DEMOCRACY

KALMAN H. SILVERT

THE VIKING PRESS   NEW YORK

First published in 1977 by The Viking Press
625 Madison Avenue, New York, N.Y. 10022
Published simultaneously in Canada by
The Macmillan Company of Canada Limited

LIBRARY OF CONGRESS CATALOGING IN PUBLICATION DATA
Silvert, Kalman H.
The reason for democracy.

1. Democracy.   I. Title.
JC423.S555   321.8   76-50597
ISBN 0-670-59059-2.

Printed in the United States of America
Set in VIP Primer

Portions of Chapter 3 are based on a chapter,
"The Kitsch in Hemispheric Realpolitik,"
by Kalman H. Silvert reprinted from
*Latin America: The Search for a
New International Role*, Vol. 1,
Latin American International Affairs Series
(R. G. Hellman and H. J. Rosenbaum, editors)
© 1975, pp. 27–38 by permission of the
publishers, Sage Publications, Inc.

to Lou—another brother

When we consider the nature and the theory of our institutions of government, the principles upon which they are supposed to rest, and review the history of their development, we are constrained to conclude that they do not mean to leave room for the play and action of purely personal and arbitrary power. Sovereignty itself is, of course, not subject to law, for it is the author and the source of law; but in our system, while sovereign powers are delegated to the agencies of government, sovereignty itself remains with the people, by whom and for whom all government exists and acts. And the law is the definition and limitation of power.

Yick Wo *v* Hopkins
118 U.S. 356, 1886

PROLOGUE

In 1893 my parents came to the golden land. The
metal they sought was not in mountains, in the
beds of streams, or in banks. What drove them
was their need to escape from tyranny into the
sun of freedom. They knew that they were fated
to carry the old ways into the new, that their acceptance in America would be hampered by
themselves as well as by their hosts. It was
through their children that they hoped the fullness of the American experience would be
realized, their own migration made complete. My
father often spoke of his five children as his "insurance," as his guarantee that the pain and joy
of taking on a new culture would find its reward
in us. I am grateful to them for their choice. But
in at least one basic way they limited my own
choices: I do not think I could live, physically
survive, in a totalitarian state. For helping me to
understand that self-respect and dignity are of

greater worth than mere survival, I thank them and I thank the tradition in which I have lived.

But I worry. I used to delight in attaching bouquets of miniature flags to the radiator emblem of our car. Now young people whose democratic integrity and courage I deeply admire have no emotional reaction to that major symbol of love of country. Instead, it has come to be a decoration on blue uniforms. It used to be unthinkable to me that a respectable person might refuse to bear arms in defense of his country. Now I regret the action but sympathize with the motives of some of those who refused the call to an Asian war. I used to think it impossible that Americans could commit atrocities, or that America's leaders would break treaties, or willfully commit common crimes in the name of political expediency. Now I am forced to know better.

I used to be convinced that America, in the fullness of its democratic example, had an important and even a key part to play in helping the entire world to a better life. I still believe that.

But I worry because American democracy is in trouble. I do not speak of economic pressures, or of crime and disorder. Democracy is in trouble because too few of us any longer understand it or its mandates, because too few of us honor it either in comprehending words or in supportive action.

As I worry I also hope, for I sense a widespread desire to return to integrity and decency in public and private affairs, and to an ordering of our civic life that would renew and renovate the democratic temper. And in addition to this reaffirmation of freedom, I also see great material potential waiting to be used. Unemployed and underutilized people, idle factories, and misused resources are a lamentable waste; but they are also a formidable fount of energy, which could help us to break out of the myth that we are condemned to an ever-increasing scarcity of goods and an ever-decreasing need for our full numbers. I have hope, because I still see in democracy what my parents saw—a just, organizing principle, a practical way of mustering social strength, and an ethically proper way of living everyday life.

I have written this book in defense of and in explanation of this vision. The form I have chosen is that of debate and argumentation—a polemic in which I try to bring as much of my professional training to bear as I can, but in the service of a political argument. I see freedom as an organizing concept, and democracy as a synthesizing system, as a total ordering of disparate and otherwise disjointed parts, so my polemic must often double back on itself. I must seem to repeat myself, and my chapters may appear in places to stand by themselves while yet obviously depending on each other. The reason is that in each chapter I try to view a separate aspect of a situation which I am always attempting to reveal in its wholeness. To my mind democracy itself is a process for creating completeness—it is not a thing, but a way of doing. I cannot analyze it, break it into parts, fondle its pieces; that would shatter its essence. Its relevance and practicality lie in its being a synthesis that reveals itself only dynamically, only *as it works*. There is no such thing as a democracy stock-still, for democracy is a way of ordering elements in the process of change itself.

This book, then, is a set of variations on a single theme. The first chapter begins the argument by choosing sides, always necessary in a polemic. Partisanship must pervade the entire book, of course. The second chapter deals with the normative and structural changes that have developed since the establishment of the Republic. The clash between democratic and undemocratic ideals and between private interest and public welfare described in that chapter provides a foundation for all the succeeding ideas. The third chapter concerns itself with the behavior of our government overseas, where it acts under only minimal legal and political constraints. This chapter adds yet another strand that runs throughout the argument—the impracticality and inefficacy of tyranny, of unaccountable power. The fourth chapter turns to the domestic situation in terms of changing technology, ongoing debates about the "governability" of democracy, the ostensible threats of population growth, the new machinery, and so on. But I also deal here with the democratic promise of an educated citizenry, and the positive effects of making rulers accountable for their actions. In sum, then, the fourth chapter describes the eminent practicality of democracy—which is yet another strand that is woven through the entire discussion. And, finally, I attempt to gather the four preceding chapters into a grand synthesis in which all the themes and counterthemes play themselves out, sometimes even against some of the same examples used elsewhere in different contexts.

I trust this approach will be intriguing, not wearisome or puzzling. It may even give the lie to the belief that to take one step to the left or another to the right totally changes one's understanding of reality. The steps I have taken are designed to show the fullness of one whole reality, and to enrich the understanding of examples by showing them as they cast shadows of differing lengths and intensities of color, depending on the angle from which light is thrown on them.

Because I am writing not only a polemic about democracy, but also what I hope is a democratic polemic—a democratically political act in itself—I have not hesitated to reveal my idiosyncratic self when I thought such casting aside of shame would help honesty of expression and clarity of thought. I have also tried to be blunt, but without being gratuitously hurtful. Courtesy, too, is a democratic virtue, as you shall see if you read far enough. But so is frankness.

I have nothing more to say by way of prefatory remarks. Let us argue.

—*Kalman H. Silvert*

New York City
1976

CONTENTS

THE REASON FOR DEMOCRACY

CHOOSING

1 SIDES

---

t is not true that men are born free and everywhere they are in chains. Men are born infants,
dependent and therefore unfree. As children they
grasp at certainties, at the conditions for physical
survival. Only as they become thinking animals
can they become responsible for their actions, and thus able to
free themselves from the accidents which have planted them in
the hands of their parents, their lands, and their material conditions. The United States has dedicated itself to the proposition
of helping men to become free as they attain competence. This
vision, always difficult to define let alone realize, has ever been
under attack. Never made real for everyone, it has still always
been partially true for some. The rich successes of America
have now brought this country to the point at which democratic
freedoms can be extended to all members of the society; the
ethic of the American Revolution is ours to complete. This very
ability forces us to ask whether we are willing to change the institutions which enforce partiality in our democracy, so that we
may respond socially to the inherent logic of that portion of our

1

laws and social ethic dedicated to accommodating order and freedom, person and society, and liberty and authority. To be able to make such an ultimate choice *requires* choice. The situation demands that we elect, even though that election may deny freedom.

Despite this maturation of America's potential, our formal institutions are in the hands of leaders who seem neither to understand nor to respect the promise of our situation. And therein lies the essence of our contemporary crisis. Immobilism, hesitancy, and cautious tinkering no longer are acceptable ways of holding together a half-free, half-trammeled society. When the ultimate choice is possible, those who would hold the line against the process of completing our national community must deny the very desirability of equality in freedom for all, and so deny the American ethic. Because our national community is uncompleted, we are in profound conflict. If the conflict persists, American life will continue to be severely perturbed and our weakening will inexorably bring us down.

It is neither consoling nor accurate to say that public affairs were as bad during other periods of our national history. The corruption and greed of earlier years in this century were contained by the inhibitory effects of a partially functioning structure of accountability, and were mitigated by frontiers physical, technological, and mythic. Today, accountability has broken down at all levels: the web of social life is weakened and in parts ripped.

The corrosion affects us all. Blame cannot be rested only on unions, or businessmen, or politicians, or liberals, or hardhats. Sloppy garbagemen are no more incompetent, and much less dangerous, than the self-deluding creators and managers of our crises at the top of the social pile. The Watergate burglars and their employers provide as much proof of our loss of artisanship as do carpenters who split planks with their badly driven nails. The politics of many learned professors mystify no less, and are no less moralistically authoritarian in implication, than the behavior of Bible-belt housewives on a book-burning binge. And so it goes, on and on.

These introductory paragraphs reflect hope and dismay. The hope cannot be realized without blunt frankness in assessing our situation. Let us have done with pap, with looking on either the bright or the dark side. Let us reject that fake objectivity that weighs an "on the one hand" against an "on the other" and comes to a "balanced" conclusion resting solidly on zero. Too many cling to the idea that "simple" social explanations are positive and happy ones and that complexity is bad in itself. For myself, I do not feel pessimistic, but I do feel bored and impatient. We can clean up the place—which is a highly optimistic and perhaps a foolishly optimistic statement—but we shall never do so if we start by denying the presence of the filth, the amount of it, its distribution, and the many ways it befouls us. What bores one about the situation is that the piles of dirt have been around for so long; only their extent and patterns are new.

Specifically, should we not be wearied unto neurosis with racism, with the self-serving pomposity of the privileged, with gangsterism in the unions, with fanatics who cannot distinguish politics from religion, with ignorant experts and arid professionalism, and so on and on? The insipid irrationality of this stuff has been with us all our lives. How tiring it is to hear it, and to cater to it at cocktail parties, in classrooms, and in public forums! Liberals, conservatives, Republicans, Democrats, racists, radicals of left and right—most of you are broken records, arrogantly proud of your reflexes, taken up with your senses and neglectful of your sense. If the Republic is to become tranquil and fruitful once again, you will have to change, to freshen your thoughts and your lives.

This, indeed, is a strange way to start a book written to commit a political act. Why begin by alienating? The reason is simply that some people cannot be reached; some people have become intellectual sociopaths, immune to reasoned understanding. Conservatives, liberals, and radicals all number such cripples in their ranks. They differ among themselves in the content of their lunacy, but not in their basic style.

For instance, there is the flag-waving conservative who believes that it is disloyal to point out flaws in America, who thinks that "bad people" are somehow besmirching a social order that otherwise would function in the manner originally ordained by God. Needless to say, such ideas have little in common with

3

those of the gentlemen who first forged the Union. True, they had a mistrustful view both of man and of man's institutions, but they also thought that social arrangements could promote the good and prevail over the flaws in human character. Writing of *The Federalist*, the late conservative political scientist Clinton Rossiter commented, "It is . . . the cold-eyed yet ultimately hopeful view of mankind that lifts *The Federalist* into the circle of classics in political theory. No one can read these pages without being reminded powerfully of both the light and dark sides of human nature—of man's capacity for reason and justice that makes free government possible, of his capacity for passion and injustice that makes it necessary." [1] If you believe in this ultimately optimistic dialectic, then we can go on. But if you are the kind of conservative who believes that hierarchy is naturally ordained, that the state is inherently bad but that we ought to worship its role as provider of national security, and that private enterprise automatically converts selfishness into the public weal—if you think in those ways, then we cannot speak to one another in our mutually incomprehensible languages. And that would be sad, a breakdown of the community essential to full freedom.

The tiresome liberal myth is that all people are essentially alike and somewhere in their souls equally "good." Therefore dishonesty, thievery, and illogic can be cured by tinkering with what people think and with one or another institutional gimmick. True, the writers of the American Constitution thought that only through enlightening men within proper institutional orders could the latent ills of man and society be contained. But they also thought that at times fundamental structural change has to be undertaken; sometimes reform is not enough and only revolution will do. As Bernard Bailyn, a liberal American historian, has written,

The colonists universally agreed that man was by nature lustful, that he was utterly untrustworthy in power, unable to control his passion for domination. The antinomy of power and liberty was accepted as the central fact of politics, and with it the belief that power was aggressive, liberty passive, and that the duty of free men was to protect the latter and constrain the former. Threats to government, it was believed, lurked everywhere, but nowhere more dangerously than in the designs of ministers in office to aggrandize power by the corrupt uses of influence, and by this means ultimately to destroy the balance of the constitution. . . .[2]

If you are the kind of liberal who agrees that sometimes men in power seek to betray the total system of democracy, and if you understand that some competing ideas cannot be blurred into compromise, then our discussion can continue. If, however, you stubbornly believe that all men are truly brothers, that the state is naturally benign but welcome to do anything in defense of the national security, and that welfare-statism can balance off monopoly and class-based privilege—if you think in those ways then we cannot speak to one another in our mutually incomprehensible social languages. And that, again, would be a saddening breakdown of community.

In other words, arguing politics with some people has, regrettably, become useless. Certainly they remain political participants—part of the problem but no part of the solution. Just as surely, too, they may be good parents and prepare tasty barbecues. Still, if they are nonreasoning types about public affairs, they will be able to read this book only if they develop a taste for entering into debate. This work is an effort to think through our present situation, and, if we are agreed to debate, to make explicit the standards by which I judge politics and thus what I propose as issues for prime public consideration. This task demands self-identification, which is achieved in part by deciding on what one is not.

It has recently become all too apparent that there are very few experts in political matters. Our highest public leaders turn out to have very few secrets, very little more information on which to base their judgments than any reasonably well-informed citizen. Our economists are of little use in telling us how simultaneously to contain inflation and prevent sustained unemployment. Our social scientists predicted only a decade ago that racial and student dissent would not or could not occur in this land. Therefore, this book is written not so much out of my scholarly activities as out of a strong urge to exercise my citizenship, to say what I think about the country which is my basic emotional concern. In this realm—which involves taste and style and personal preference—none of us needs feel that those who rule are more refined in their sensibilities than those who are ruled. On the contrary, it may well be that the salt of power swamps the senses of those who have too much of it.

Whatever our station, and whether we are gross or cultured in our tastes, we all choose a way, an idea of the preferable over the undesirable. The nature of the choice is crucial, of course, for some choices condemn the chooser to poverty of spirit and a restriction of further choice—to the loss of public life itself.

Not only the individual man but also the state has to choose its demon. That is the great and revolutionary principle of Plato's *Republic*. Only by choosing a "good demon" can a state secure its eudaimonia, its real happiness. We cannot leave the attainment of this goal to mere chance, nor can we hope to find it by a stroke of luck. In social life as well as in individual life rational thought must take the leading part. It must show us the way and illuminate the way from the first to the last step. The welfare of a state is not its increase in physical power. The desire to have "more and more" is just as disastrous in the life of a state as in individual life. If the state yields to this desire, that is the beginning of its end. The enlargement of its territory, the superiority over its neighbors, the advance in its military or economic power, all this cannot avert the ruin of the state but rather hastens it. The self-preservation of the state cannot be secured by its material prosperity nor can it be guaranteed by the maintenance of certain constitutional laws. Written constitutions or legal charters have no real binding force, if they are not the expression of a constitution that is written in the citizens' minds. Without this moral support the very strength of a state becomes its inherent danger.[3]

The implications of the above passage have moved me throughout my reasoning life. The ideas are also consonant with much that motivated the framers of our political system: social will resides in the governed; consensus matters; we have the power to make up and to change our minds and thereby part of the world's essence; the spirit of affairs is important, and we can change it. Another inference is that the "good demons" can be corralled through the exercise of individual creativity, thus that there is need in this world for the particularity of the unique. Obviously, then, social life is both satisfying and beneficent to the extent to which it allows room for the play of unique and yet necessarily social minds. Indeed, what other kind of mind can there be?

The most discouraging aspect of the pass we have come to is that the freedom and responsibility prescribed as good in our basic national documents and taught to us in our schools are at direct odds with all too much of our national practice. When Richard Nixon referred to the American people as children, he was expressing himself on the proper role of the elite, and making a statement directly subversive of the concepts underlying the American Constitution. It is not for children to reason, to be understanding of others, to live in secular and relativistic community. They must be cajoled, taught, guided, led—but never helped to construct their own realities, to assume the creative part of the citizen-building culture in an ever-expanding world of ideas, appreciations, discriminations, and perceptions. If the nature of man is to remain a child, then let us dispense with democracy, a political order that demands maturity for its maintenance. And, of course, let us also cast aside any ideas that education creates the preconditions for freedom, and instead merely train mechanics. What such as Nixon are telling us, of course, is that our educations are worthless to our personalities, our citizenship a sham, our expertness to be used merely as advertisement to sell preestablished conclusions.

We cannot pretend that those authoritarian strictures for our diminution have not partially worked. They have. And as a consequence many of us have sometimes acted incompetently without even knowing it, have often voted in sterile and mechanical fashion bereft of meaningful choice, and have all too often been partriotic for our state but unwittingly disloyal to our nation. Examples abound of these belittlings of mind, dignity, and citizenship. For instance, I am often asked by government officials to advise them on international politics. But they withhold information, lie, fool themselves and others, and listen so selectively with the ears of their superiors that one can have no certainty of the "facts" or of precision of expression. Under such conditions, an "expert" can merely write footnotes to someone else's prejudices.

As for voting, we all know that both parties have become empty, unable to winnow candidates and issues. They are understood as unresponsive and inefficacious by a clear majority of Americans, who increasingly are falling back into local politics

7

and are unable to muster meaningful consensual agreement on national questions. Now that many more registered Americans stay home in bi-elections than vote, we are approaching the *voto en blanco*—the blank vote—the abstentionist electoral behavior of many a pseudo-democracy abroad.

And as for loyalty, let me give a personal example. I remember with shame and chagrin the public speeches I have given arguing that the Central Intelligence Agency had little to do with the Chilean revolution of September 11, 1973. In the absence of facts, I was substituting my reason—suggesting that things were so bad in Chile in any event that the CIA had little reason to intervene. In other words, I was ascribing more sense to that agency than it had. And, like so many of my fellow citizens, I found it difficult to believe that the black arts were a routinely accepted part of U.S. foreign policy. The "bottom line" of that nonthinking, that inexpertness, that incompetence is that I contributed to maintaining the reputation of my formal governors but was of disservice to my nation as a whole. I unintentionally betrayed my education and my fellow citizens, who had conjointly made it possible for me to gain that education and acceptance. I was put into a position in which support of the state became disloyalty to community. Any political mechanism that casts its citizens into such a crisis of morality, competence, and loyalty is self-defeating, and subversive of its own continuity. To continue in power it must substitute overt coercion for the willing acceptance it has lost. As Cassirer put it in the last sentence of the passage above, "the very strength" of such a state "becomes its inherent danger." *

---

* My interpretation of the Enlightenment, and of many other aspects of political thought after Machiavelli, relies heavily on the works of Ernst Cassirer. Therefore, I have been faced with something of a scholarly dilemma in quoting from Rousseau, Montesquieu, and others. To go directly back to the original works may suggest that the selection of given cited passages was my own or that the interpretation was my own creation. The ethical course is to stay with the interpretive works in my citations, for I would rather be accused of laziness than of dishonesty. My reliance on Cassirer is not idiosyncratic. As Peter Gay has pointed out (in "The Social History of Ideas: Ernst Cassirer and After," in Kurt H. Wolff and Barrington Moore, Jr., eds., *The Critical Spirit,* 1967, p. 116) ". . . for the most part Cassirer's Rousseau is today the Rousseau of the scholars."

Jean-Jacques Rousseau, an inspirer of many of the founders of the Republic, would not have been at all surprised by this interplay between education and citizenship on one hand and incompetence and alienation on the other. He saw it as in the nature of man to strive for reasoned understanding, and in the nature of social life as he knew it to attempt to deprive him of that understanding. I agree entirely with this view of the situation. My most profound reason for embarking on this essay, then, is that I think it in my nature, and in that of all men, to create their understandings of the world. Together with our world of "things," these constructions become social reality, the stuff of which states, communities, or any social universe are built. The primacy of this idea in political thought is not a new notion, of course. Montesquieu, who suggested the architectonic structure of the American government, put it this way: "The corruption of every government begins almost always with the corruption of its principles. . . . Once the principles of a government are corrupt the best laws become bad and turn against the state; when the principles are healthy, bad laws have the effect of good ones. The force of the principle carries everything with it. . . ." [4] The *philosophes* of the Enlightenment argued that right thinking was the precondition for right action. Rousseau put the same idea more historically and instrumentally, and thus in a way that is dismayingly appropriate to our own times:

The wounds the existing structure of society has inflicted on mankind cannot be healed by destroying the instrument that caused them. We must look further; we must attack not the instrument but the hand that guided it. It is not the form of the social contract as such that is at fault; it is rather the will that inspires the contract. So long as that will is bound to the service of individuals or groups that have gained special privilege through power or wealth, it is the source of all evil, the champion and protector of all the suffering and injustice that men can inflict on one another. [5]

To sum up, then, my basic purpose in writing this book is to perform an act of creative understanding. My second purpose is

---

Cassirer must be exempted from blame for my extrapolations from his work, of course, for I am putting him to use in historical and social-scientific applications and thus removing him from his own realm of philosophy.

to try to put myself back into one piece, to make my citizenship coherent with my intellectual formation. My third has not yet been explicitly mentioned, but it is obvious: I want to be free of the untoward exactions of others. We are all tired of being ripped off by tax collectors, politicians, businessmen, public utilities companies, repairmen, and shoeshine boys. Clearly, a book or a primordial scream will do little to get these monkeys off our shoulders. But maybe, maybe a little reasoning will help.

My method here will be to reason aloud. My procedure will be to construct a diagnosis, from which prescription may suggest itself. In justifying this reasoning process through a diagnostic scheme, let me call again on the Enlightenment for help.

The power of reason does not consist in enabling us to transcend the empirical world but rather in teaching us to feel at home in it. . . . Reason is now [in the 18th century] looked upon rather as an acquisition than as a heritage. It is not the treasury of the mind in which the truth like a minted coin lies stored; it is rather the original intellectual force which guides the discovery and determination of truth. This determination is the seed and the indispensable presupposition of all real certainty. The whole eighteenth century understands reason in this sense; not as a sound body of knowledge, principles, and truths, but as a kind of energy, a force which is fully comprehensible only in its agency and effects. What reason is, and what it can do, can never be known by its results but only by its function. . . . Only in this two-fold intellectual movement can the concept of reason be fully characterized, namely, as a concept of agency, not of being.[6]

So it was that the Founding Fathers saw reason, too, and that is why they also saw a constitution as establishing social settings that can promote the exercise of reason. The long life of the document itself is the best evidence of the wisdom of the original perception—reason not as a fixed body of knowledge, not as an inheritance coming to us in a lump from the past, but as a functioning force, a way of judging, the structure of thought from which might flow the ethically proper social will, that set of motivations which might promote the public weal.

Machiavelli, too, implied the importance of the reasoning mind, although without the Enlightenment's explicit ethic. Machiavelli was the first to wring the sacred out of the secular, and to promote thought to a sovereign position in the mundane world of the state. He argued that diagnosis, the understanding of a situation, was the first step on the road to political salvation. Political thought was, for him, analogous to the diagnosis, prognosis, and therapy practiced by physicians. Because the diagnosis governs the prognosis and therapy, it is primary, of course. If the diagnosis is incorrect, the patient's case becomes hopeless. "So it happens in political bodies; for when the evils and disturbances that may probably arise in any government are foreseen, which yet can only be done by a sagacious and provident man, it is easy to ward them off; but if they are suffered to sprout up and grow to such a height that their malignity is obvious to every one, there is seldom any remedy to be found of sufficient efficacy to repress them." [7]

In the United States our very conceptions of the polity and of civil society are at issue. The fragmentation of our life-situations forces us to rethink not only our times, but also the origins of our period. We shall have to understand and then transcend the Enlightenment to create a harmonious future. Diagnostically, then, we are working not on a common cold but on a life-threatening malady. If this suspicion is correct, then the analogy of the physician breaks down. The healer may not judge the moral value of the being he is helping; it may not matter to him whether he is saving the life of devil or saint. But political men are both the sick and the healers, and whether the body politic on which they are working is for them good or bad is, of course, the very point of their actions. When ultimate beliefs about public life are in play, then ultimate judgment also enters. The very kind of people we are becomes a dynamic element in the schema. Because judgment is unavoidable under such conditions, so too are destruction and creation.

If we are actually in the agony of ultimate choice, then any choice—one we may like or one we may despise—implies many and deep changes in our social order. We will not move into a totalitarian dictatorship, for example, without breaking many heads and many institutions. Nor will we deepen and extend our democracy without profoundly changing our system of rewards, our judgments of individual worth, and our ways of forcing accountability on public institutions. The only certainty is that we cannot choose to do nothing, for we are already in a pervasive irrationality that satisfies neither the dark nor the light sides of our desires. We are not at a crossroads where we can camp; we are on a freeway at rush hour.

THE AMERICAN REVOLUTIONARY ETHIC AND ITS BETRAYAL

here is no good reason to think of any society as a "system." There are many bad ones, though, all based on argument by analogy. For example, in the Land of the Automobile it is tempting to imagine the country as a big car that needs oil and gas (inputs), burns up fuel (the "transformation" functions that go on in the mysterious black box), and delivers movement, breezes, sex, and deaths (outputs), although not without sometimes coughing so that we know we must turn to a mechanic (feedback). Before the automobile age, our predecessors often compared society to the human body. Anyone can think up organic analogies, so I leave to the reader his own fun in fitting anatomical pieces to social functions and roles.

These machinelike pictures of society suggest that the measure of the socially good is the harmonious consistency of interlocked parts linked in a "drive-train" to perform a single cluster of functions. That is a value judgment, a statement of what society *should* be, with which I will not argue here, although I strongly disagree. But as a guide to gross understanding, let alone to refined prediction, the vision is nonsense. People are just not that way. Happily, we probably cannot be made to be that way, either.

In our daily lives the world buffets us in capricious, arbitrary, uneven, and unpredictable ways. Cancer strikes whom it will, computers malfunction with exquisite randomness, weather forecasters rarely beat the odds, and so it goes. Despite what we all know, our political and scientific image-makers insist that the world is self-regulating, trying to find a happy medium. Most of us like to think of society as a stable thing in which parts interact without friction. The human bits are made up of "statuses" and "roles," but not of whole bodies and personalities. The machine analogy fails because a person is not a "part." People engage in play and innovation in their interactions and—also unlike machine parts—they invent and otherwise try to act originally. Granted, it is easier to "replace" an "individual" in a "status" than to fire a person. Still, it is a human being who finds himself out of work, not a replaceable part that is being discarded.

If we try to understand ourselves only analytically, bit by bit and piece by piece, then the differences among us will stand out. Disorder is what will appear, and we shall have to decide whether the disorder is creative or destructive. Pure analysis will lead us to see all societies as inconsistent, contradictory, disjointed, and disjunctive—words we have been taught to shudder at, for they ostensibly describe "instability." However, it is really obvious that any piecemeal look at social life can reveal only a jumble—that is normality, a statement I make without trace of irony or disapproval. But that social pieces do not fit neatly together does not imply that societies are chaotic. On the contrary, they all have some coherent sense, or sets of coherent senses. Only in the construction of the whole can we find such significance, not in assuming some universal meaning inherent in each piece. The *synthesis* of a situation, the way it is put together, is qualitatively different from the pieces of which it is composed. A systems-analogy will not serve this way of understanding, for while the synthesis of a machine is only the fitting together of its parts, a social synthesis is the creation of meanings used to make one element of life serve, complement, or contradict another. Overarching social understandings include the comprehension that direct contradictories are always part of a single situation. To put it simply, order in social life is found not in the interaction of parts, but in thinking arrangements into existence.

In this view of social life, there is no sense in criticizing American politics because it contains contradictions. One should expect a gulf, for example, between what politicians say they are doing and what they actually are doing. If the gap is created by outright lying, then we have an outrageous attack on the commonality of understanding necessary for democratic politics. But if genuine differences in intellectual ability and perceptions are involved, then we are merely dealing with the nature of things. Thus, it is normal and even necessary that, duplicity aside, later generations will see selfishness and generosity at odds within groups of persons who, at the time, thought they were being entirely consistent. An obvious case concerns the men who wrote the Declaration of Independence and the American Constitution. Were they children of the Enlightenment, searching for freedom to follow the teachings of science and reason, avid to liberate minds to live in conformity with nature and nature's laws? Or were they merely the spokesmen of their own class interests, pursuing their advantage as they saw fit? A vulgar interpretation would make the following two statements mutually exclusive:

My theme can be put simply and succinctly . . . It is this: that the Old World imagined the Enlightenment and the New World realized it; America absorbed it, reflected it, and institutionalized it.[1]

. . . the concept of the Constitution as a piece of abstract legislation reflecting no group interests and recognizing no economic antagonisms is entirely false. It was an economic document drawn with superb skill by men whose property interests were immediately at stake; and as such it appealed directly and unerringly to identical interests in the country at large.[2]

One need have no difficulty in understanding both statements as historically and simultaneously valid, for there is no reason that two truths cannot occupy the same space. Today, however, the situation is different, for through a historical process stemming from the constitutional innovators, the particularities of economic interest are threatening to the democratic comity which two centuries ago was thought to be crucial to the enlargement of both political and economic rationality. The people who made possible both modern capitalism and the present crisis of democracy saw some of the dangers in the infiltration of economic power into the political mechanism. But they could no more have understood all the anomalies inherent in their own postulations than they could control the unborn generations of their heirs. As it was, they did what all men do: They attempted to work out a social arrangement which would be in their perceived interest. That statement is hardly shocking, surprising, or reprehensible. The important issue, of course, is how they perceived that interest, and how they related techniques to the achievement of their interested goals.

They attempted to accommodate the differing ways of economics and politics by designing two different structures, having in common built-in but different systems of accountability. The economic system was to be held in check by competition; self-equilibration would come from striving actors seeking private gain in a public manner, constrained by the similar activities of other individuals. And the state was to be held in check by the division of powers, by the system of checks and balances, and by the geographical spread of the national state—by its very size, it would have to embrace a plurality of competing interests, imperfectly replicating in the political arena the competitiveness of the economic marketplace.

Another idea also tied the economic and political orders: the notion that man was creator of economic value as well as of his worldly social situation. Most of us have been solemnly told by many a teacher that the Declaration of Independence was a "radical" document because it talked of "life, liberty, and the pursuit of happiness," but that the Constitution was conservative because it changed the words to "life, liberty, and property." There is a difference, of course, but it is not nearly so great as that which suggests itself to modern minds. To read Locke is to learn that the prevailing theory of value when the Constitution was written was the Liberal version of the labor theory of value. That is, that the value of a good or a service is given it by its infusion with human labor. In the famous example, an acorn lying on the ground has no value. The act of stooping to pick it up and carry it to market imbues it with worth, which derives only from the human effort expended. So, the implication of the constitutional prohibition against depriving anyone of his property without due process of law is that such deprivation necessarily also strips from the person the liberty he exercised in creating the value of his property and, by further extension, that part of his life and character which he lent to his efforts.*

The contemporary mind in this country uses a different theory of value, one based on the mechanics of market exchanges. In this view, labor is simply another item entering into market transactions; like any other commodity, labor must obey the "laws" of supply and demand. An unused plant is *economically* the same as an unemployed machinist. In such an approach, life, liberty, and property become totally separate concepts. "Life" is narrowed to physical questions involving imprisonment and execution; "liberty" is the avoidance of constraint; "property" is what one owns. A harmonious triad has cracked into three separate and discordant notes.

This example illustrates historical changes in the way we create relations among the facets of our life. When differences among major areas of social life become so great that one or another must change its very structure and character, then no stretches of imagination or symbol-making can hold things together. We must change the institutions, or become socially psychotic.

Two great contradictions are at the breaking point in American life. One concerns a primary clash in world views—the distance that increasingly separates original Liberal ideas from the evolution of Utilitarian thought as both are complicated by still other opposing ideas. And the other concerns the structure of our political community, the increasing irreconcilability between citizenship and privilege, between nation and social class. Again, these oppositions should not be thought of crudely, as the product of hypocritical men fooling the multitudes while

* Locke says as much in his Second Treatise: He explains men's purpose of entering into a social compact as being for "the mutual preservation of their lives, liberties and estates, which I call by the general name—property."

they line their pockets. Certainly there have been and are such cynical manipulators. But, we should view these contradictions as evolving naturally, for they are inherent to patterns of thought and structure in all nations that have experienced democratic, capitalist, Protestant-influenced, national development. All such countries have to decide whether they want integrated community and democracy, or class privilege and totalitarianism.

Liberalism, Utilitarianism, and Their Derivatives To rest content with calling the American revolutionaries children of the Enlightenment is hardly clarifying. It would have been a wise child of the 1780s who could have known that to be an offspring of Voltaire or of Rousseau was to be either a toad or a fairy prince. The French *philosophes* and Locke, the English philosopher who so powerfully influenced the new nation-builders, thought in common about such issues as freedom, the proper forms of political organization, the difference between a sovereign and sovereignty, and a certain atomic view of man. They also shared the necessity for thinking through how to explain the revolutionary situation of Europe, and how to construct a new world which would encompass Newtonian physics, a secular ethics, the rising bourgeoisie, and those other elements which were to eventuate in amazing bursts of social energy which have lasted to our own time. But even the Enlightenment thinkers, so early in the modern game, divided along lines which still perplex and influence us. For example, Locke and his Utilitarian successors (Bentham, the Mills, and others) all thought that man learned only from experience. He was born with a *tabula rasa* and learned by living, in effect. Rousseau, however, tentatively explored radically different possibilities, to which Kant gave philosophical form and much further elaboration. They both turned inward, holding that the creation of understanding came from *within* man, not from experience working on him from the outside. The division between the two schools of thought becomes apparent when one deals with the question of freedom. Locke the Liberal and his Utilitarian successors defined freedom as essentially an absence of constraint, the "outside" not interfering with the "inside." For Rousseau, however, freedom came from within man, and was measured by his ability to realize himself in his nature. Many later thinkers deem both constructions incorrect because they posit a false division between the personal and the social, the individual and the cultural. We need not enter further into this discussion here, for this argumentation could not have been apparent to the American colonists. The waves of the ocean they swam in were obvious enough; the cross-currents were too subtle to detect. As it was, in the last quarter of the eighteenth century they made a set of choices which took concrete form in the Constitution. The structure of thought of that document, while later evidently modified, redefined, understood variously, and misunderstood, still exercises powerful legal and social influences on our daily political life. The motivating world view of the revolutionary founders, however, underwent mighty changes within a few years of the promulgation of the Constitution: their revolutionary Liberalism began to be diluted by a conservatizing Utilitarianism, making it harder and harder to reconcile the spirit of the laws with the applications they were given. The theoretical base line for the independence period must be drawn from Locke, the most immediate and powerful influence on American minds. Morton White writes:

. . . For more than a century—from the time that [Jonathan] Edwards as a young man pored over Locke's *Two Treatises of Government,* and up to the days when Emerson was dismissing Locke as a prosaic mind—that deep, sober, thoroughly honest, and often inconsistent Englishman was at the center of American philosophical attention. He provided Americans with views to be canonized as well as views to be condemned, and he constructed a framework and language within which much of their thinking took place even when he did not make converts of them. Most importantly for our purposes, he developed a theory of scientific knowledge that had enormous impact on American thought about religion, morals, law, and politics. That theory helps us to understand one of the dominant features of American thought—its celebration of, and frequent appeal to, a power of the mind called "intuition." One of the most striking characteristics of American thought in this period was a tendency to appeal to forms of immediate insight into truth, like Edwards' Sense of the Heart, the intuition of self-evident principles in the Declaration of Independence, and Emerson's Reason. . . .[3]

I have quoted this at length in order to explore a few of the implications of that phrase we all know, "We hold these truths to be self-evident, that all men are created equal. . . ." Very few Americans would subscribe any longer to that statement, as many public opinion polls attest. Worse, very few Americans any longer understand what it means or have any notion of its intellectual origins. A famous American lawyer recently shrugged off the idea of equality with the shallow statement, "We all know that people are unequal—some are smart, some dumb, some ugly, some pretty." The person went on, "I don't agree with the idea of equality." Of course, those who argued for the concept of equality over two centuries ago did not "believe" in it in the sense in which the learned lawyer was using it, either. They also knew perfectly well not only that some people are smarter or fairer than others, but also that some are better placed than others. Their postulation of the idea of equality was entirely different.

The importance of the concept of self-evident truths is that it was employed to establish a science of morality as well as of astronomy and physics. Locke and his followers, "empiricists" all, held that certain learning from experience revealed truth and falsity in the act of perception. Red is not green; motion is not stillness; life is not death. From self-evident "truths" can be constructed a set of axioms concerning ethical and moral matters as well as those describing the physical universe. Locke himself was ambivalent about the self-evident nature of moral axioms, but there was little hesitation about adopting the idea on the part of the practical political revolutionaries in the American colonies. The equality of man which they understood intuitively as true did not refer to his personal endowments or his social prestige, *but rather to his condition as a human being.* In the nature of his being, man was born not to live in sacredly ordained and sanctioned subordination, but only in freely assented and limited social constraint, to that minimum required for stability and security. People should join in a compact only of a certain kind: that kind required to escape from arbitrary control. "This freedom from absolute, arbitrary power is so necessary to, and closely joined with, a man's preservation, that he cannot part with it but by what forfeits his preservation and life altogether." [4]

The *revolutionary* point to this is that *all* men *equally* should have a right to enjoy life and make of it what they can. Therefore, no sacred claim to special status on the part of a monarch may be entertained. The *constitutional* point is that in a secular world respecting no claims to unique status, all men must be of equal status before the laws. The *moral* point is that all institutions, to be judged "good," must function in harmony with self-evident truths concerning the nature of man. Naturally, the boundaries of these concepts are in dispute and, indeed, make up much of the content of constitutional law. For example, the sacred and the secular are still confused in such areas as education, or concerning such issues as abortion and euthanasia. And executives—even vice-presidents—claim special legal treatment and powers by investing national security with God-given purpose. As for equality before the laws, should the same law apply equally to all persons, or to special classes of persons? Should the law be unequally applied in order to foment equality, as in aid to the sick, the lame, and the halt? [5] And as for "natural law," through what agencies can we ascertain specifically what it is? How do we equate "natural" law with the "positive" law which courts must apply? Even Locke was contradictory on the subject of whether moral "principles" were self-evident and thus axiomatic, so how can we expect better in the confusion of modern times?

But these disquisitions obscure the task of the constitutionalist revolutionaries: the establishment of a political system to free men by providing for their security, in accord with rationalistic ideas of the unity of physical and moral "science," and through the agency of institutions whose relative ethical value could be measured against the absolute standards of "nature." In this construction the concept of equality has very specific meanings. It is *polemically* useful in arguing against the special claims of divinely inspired monarchs and in favor of the regular succession of citizens to political posts. It is *scientifically* useful in claiming that in certain respects all persons boil down to the same kind of unit, that therefore scientific "law" holds for all and the atomic theories of Newton can work for society as for physics. And it is *politically* useful in creating a community through which to express the "general will" from which flows all governmental authority. Combined, these ideas permitted the development of a constitutional document designed to allow the proper working of a process of adjustment to nature. The document could be short, because it expressed an ethical view of social life which, as it was used, would spin out its own elaboration. It would complete its own creation, as societies themselves were meant to do.

Nothing is more important about the Constitution than the statement that it concerns institutional orders and relations held in an ethical frame within a political community. I speak here not of the logic of the supporting ideas, the philosophical sophistication of the reasoning, or the self-interest of the writers of the document, but rather of the style of thought, the construction of the ideas themselves. In this area, there is little dispute. To wit, and in recapitulation:

· The document is an elaboration of purportedly self-evidently true propositions.

· It posits social equality as a primal condition of all men, and derives from that proposition a secular, contained, limited political authority.

· It assumes that the purpose of the state is, in effect, to supply the police powers and, more broadly, to ensure citizens in the stability and security of their lives as members of a political nation.

· It leaves it to citizens otherwise to work out their destinies, and attempts to promote the use of reason by civil libertarian guarantees.

· It clearly establishes the separateness of the political order from the economic and religious realms; but for the purposes of politics, it is firm in removing religion as a criterion of citizenship, while sadly hedging on economic power, as is clearly evident in its acceptance of slavery.

· It attempts to design a formal governmental structure which will be self-regulating through the division of powers and the effects of national scope; it assumes that the same end of self-governance will work through the economic market.

Looking at the document this way reveals that it emphasizes not *individuals,* but how *persons* can become members of a political community and work out their nature through institutional conduct infused with an ethical content. The constitutionalists' "natural law" thus refers not simply to the nature of discrete persons, not only to "naturally good" ways of institutional action, but to the interaction of the two, so that the nature of the person and the nature of social life can be mutually enriching—or, to put it another way, so that the public and private welfare can become one.

Now we can understand better what was meant by equality in this classical concept. What is equal for all men is their nature; what is equal for all institutions is their "naturally" proper functioning; what is an equal goal for all is the reconciliation of the naturalness of the person and the naturalness of his institutions. Thus, *it is only in respect to their position vis-a-vis authority and the rules of the total social game that men are naturally equal,* and thus *should be* equal in actual fact.

This concept has lost most of its idealistic richness because it has been diluted into the statement that all men are merely equal before the laws. True, the original statement of the Liberal idea is unclear because later distinctions among government, state, and nation were not yet needed, and the Liberals were obviously dealing with a problem involving the total construction of community. They were witness to the death of an old order and the building of a new one. They were making not only new governments, but new communities. The rules before which they thought men should be equal are those concerning the integrity of community; the Founding Fathers were in the first instance *nation*-builders, not *republic*-builders.

For two hundred years the European culture world has been trying to get away from the consequences of this postulation: that people should be citizens in communities of universal membership. The idea that man makes his own value and his own social orders, before which he is equal in rights, is incompatible with the idea that the formal organ of the nation—the state—should engage in a balancing act, express the will of this or that competing interest group, become the referee if not the expression of the raw power of elites. The classically Liberal state is designed to ensure *all* citizens in their equal status. The corrupted Liberal state seeks only to ensure all citizens in the equal application of laws, which are the fallout of the interplay of special interests—and usually it does not do that job overly well, either. In the classical way of thinking, the construction of a *total* political community is the necessary precondition for equality in that community; once such equality has been established, particular positions within the community may be taken. There is a more popular way to put it: The Liberal ideal was the establishment of equality of political condition. Thereafter, equality of individual opportunity could have its day. To have followed this precept would have meant a different relation between class and nation than we now have, and would similarly have obviated the tortured ideological games that have been played for the past two centuries in the attempt to twist away from this socialized concept of equality.

Let us turn first to the destruction of Liberal thought, and then to the structural strains which now threaten to tear apart our political community. But let us understand, too, that Liberal thinkers armed their own adversaries.

Utilitarianism and Scientism Between the year of the Declaration of Independence and the year of the Monroe Doctrine, the style and sense of West European culture changed profoundly and with a speed that still seems incredible. All aspects of symbolic life demonstrate this shift in outlook. In music, for example, the deaths of Mozart and Haydn, the apogee of Beethoven's career, the work of Schubert, and the appearance of the virtuoso temperament are all compressed within thirty years. Small wonder that Beethoven felt he had become demodé before the end of his life. The mechanical arts were pushed by the first production in series and a set of inventions that spurred the grand industrial changes of the age of steam. The invention of new techniques in music and in industrial production were matched in the beginnings of statistics, military innovations, and changes in universities that led to the first graduate research seminars in German universities in the 1830s. The victory of the burghers was ushering in a new world, universalist in its first claims, an earth to be open to all. But second thoughts soon set in, for the children of the newly successful had interests to defend which their revolutionary progenitors had in their lifetimes not yet made concrete.

Democratic political thought has not succeeded in repeating the intellectual victories of those heady years in which the new bourgeois states came into being. It is commonplace and accurate to say that the brilliance, dash, and intellectual virtuosity of America's first generation of revolutionary leaders has never since been equalled. Indeed, in matters dealing with the structured functioning of politics as a semi-autonomous institutional activity, it is quite safe to say that all has been downhill since the turn of the nineteenth century. Even Marx, the grandest of the social thinkers after the men of the Enlightenment, has little to say about the state in itself, and treats politics as essentially a reflection of more basic forces. One can understand why most Marxists slight politics as such, given their view of class conflict in the process of social change in capitalist societies. But why should other schools of thought have become so mechanistic, so neglectful of the grand issues only so recently raised and so tentatively, hesitantly, and uncertainly applied? The question is serious, for its answer may well be that classically Liberal communitarian democracy is a concept dangerous to established interest. A manifestation in our time of this neglect—to take only one example among very many—is that only one or two recognized academic specialists in political development in the United States see the essentials of a free polity as, in itself, defining political development. No mainstream economist does so, naturally.

The basis of a historical explanation is in that heady transition period lying roughly between 1790 and 1825. The outlines of the new class and political structures were established. Order, regularity, predictability, and science became the watchwords. The creators of the new order had been forced to ask to what ends they wished to push the changes they had forced. Further, and precisely because they quite literally were nation-builders, they had to concern themselves with the relation between new political forms and their goals. Perforce, their thinking had to be both visionary and instrumental; they had to bring their feelings into harmony with the structures of their doings. They left a world with a lot of room in it, but not unlimited space. Their celebration of reason and science in a secularized social universe opened doors for the inquiring mind. Their linking of middle and upper social groups, with a promise to the lower ones, generated wide spaces for social mobility, or just simple social climbing. Their espousal of the mechanical arts created new jobs, blew up the size of cities, expanded commerce, and allowed men to move about the physical world ever more rapidly. Steadily, however, the freedom-spaces provided by the structural thinkers of the eighteenth century were filled and, more unhappily, were even diminished by those who followed. Worse yet, the prime area of political thought which Liberals opened— the structure of democratic hope and promise—is not yet as richly furnished as when they left it. Their Utilitarian successors took only the mechanistic, encyclopedic, scientific thought of the Enlightenment, and left behind the morality of Rousseau and his admirer, Kant, and the ethical institutionalism of Locke. The Utilitarians moved into a grand mansion, took its dimensions for granted, and eventually forgot that their house was not the city of man. They confused their historical particularity with the being of all men, ending up prescribing pure social "laws," but unable to explain real behavior. The path of this progressive impoverishment of mind leads directly to our present political hollowness.

The Utilitarian view of the world is not difficult to describe. Christian Bay, an important writer on matters of freedom, lists ten distinguishing characteristics of the school, of which the first three are basic.

The philosophical premises that were adopted wholeheartedly by [Jeremy] Bentham, James Mill, and many of their followers, though not without crucial reservations by the younger [John Stuart] Mill, may be listed as follows:

1. Happiness is the only fundamental and intrinsic value. Happiness is equivalent to the sum of the pleasure minus the sum of the pain.

2. The only legitimate standard by which to evaluate social institu-

tions, and things and events in general, is their probable or demonstrable utility in promoting happiness.

3. All men are equal, in the sense that an equal amount of happiness for any two people is equally valuable. . . .[6]

The theory was intended to lead to a scientific politics, based on the ability to give numerical value to pleasures and pains. This calculus, so called, could then be brought into play to tell policymakers what decisions to make. That policy which renders the most units of pleasure and the least of pain is, clearly, what should be followed. Policy decisions then become, in essence, simply a matter of making the proper factual determinations and routinely applying the appropriate recipe. In effect, the art is taken out of politics and technics rule. Or, to put it another way, politics becomes depoliticized.

Let us not stop to search out the internal illogic of the argument. The important problem for us remains the style of thought. Utilitarianism turns away from the idea that people may find special gratifications in institutional life and toward the notion that society is but an aggregation of individuals. Each individual is moved by the desire to avoid pain and find pleasure; ergo, society as a whole is moved by similar evasions and attractions. Change is caused by the zigzags describing the movement of people away from pain and toward pleasure; and when the pain quotient mixed in with the pleasure becomes too high, the direction shifts from that form of pleasure to another, perhaps through a valley of pain. In other words, each individual is self-equilibrating and so, in direct reflection, is society. This view of cause is a very far cry from the Liberal idea that institutions that collectively promote the ability to exercise reason enable men to move *through those institutions* toward a life in conformity with nature. Classical Liberal thought is social; Utilitarian thought is asocial, vulgar psychological reductionism. But it is Utilitarianism, and not Liberalism, which has become the basis of modern microeconomics and of most other social scientific and political thought.

Coincidentally with the development of Utilitarianism, economics appropriately split away from political studies. Thus, political economy was denied by capitalist democrats, to reappear as a Marxist idea, together with the Marxist version of the labor theory of value. The study of politics fell to the discipline of history, and reemerged only slowly and hesitantly toward the end of the nineteenth century, closely allied to public administration and the development of a civil service. But economics, under the now misused label "Liberal," became micro-economics, and eventually presented itself as intellectually the "hardest" and most "scientific" of the social sciences. Indeed, so "scientific" has standard Western economics become that in Israel, for instance, the discipline is no longer linked to the social sciences, and is treated as an abstract subject, like mathematics. The Utilitarians extracted *persons* from their social settings, and made *individuals* out of them. Mainstream economists have now extracted the life out of individuals, and have made them into abstractions in an exchange equation. Such an accomplishment is not easily achieved; it takes a lot of self-mystification to accept either Utilitarianism or the prescriptions of those economists. But it is amazing how many of us manage that difficult lunacy.

The basic premises of micro-economics are virtually the same as that of Utilitarianism. Value is given to goods and services through the exchange mechanism, the marketplace. The market is inhabited by actors seeking to maximize gain (read "pleasure") and avoid loss (read "pain"). This seeking-avoidance mechanism is built into man, who is but an early version of the later developed heat-seeking missile. Reason operates only in function of that internal psychological mechanism. The marketplace that most purely and certainly permits the gain-loss dynamic to operate is also the economic scene that most rapidly promotes "development." Any purpose of the goods and services produced other than to gratify the winners is incidental—gain (read "happiness") is the goal in itself, and in itself alone.

This radical statement of the micro-economic position is not misplaced, even though most economists quail at the social costs of attempting to implement such programs, and water down their views with welfare-statism and discussions of non-economic factors or of "social impediments to economic development." As we shall see, an attempt is being made in totalitarian Chile to implement precisely a micro-economic "liberal" economy. That the result is quite literally starvation is but the "cost" of the "necessary" transition toward a more "rational" economy than the state capitalism which preceded it. That it is obviously the poor who starve is simply in the nature of things. Those who have the least power over events, who profited the least from past inflations, who have been pushed around by left and right for years—it is only natural that they should pay the highest price to repair the mistakes made by others. But, as many of my economist acquaintances put it, what else is there to do? If there is only one set of economic laws, all men respond to them to their benefit or fail to respect them to their detriment. Differing historical and social situations? Differing values? Differing purposes? Nonsense—all men are the same in their psyches, and reason had best adjust to that "fact."

The Utilitarian steel that the economists have worked into a fine Italian stiletto is not theirs alone; it becomes a sledgehammer in the hands of most of our politicians. Consider the cheapening of the word "pragmatic." In the mouths of our political leaders, it means only "practical," instead of referring to the relation between an idea and its likely, real consequences. Always linked to this vulgar usage of the word is the idea that there are "problems" somewhere "out there." Somehow, those "problems" have a life of their own. They appear by themselves, they force themselves upon us, they "demand" to be "solved." So, true to the naive empiricist theory of the Utilitarian, the political men pretend that experience is pressing in on them, denting creases in their cortexes. Because the "problems" have appeared, untouched by human mind until their perception, they "demand" solution. Since to define a problem is not a truly political act (that is, one that is normative and intellectually created), then it follows that to solve it cannot be political in that sense, either. So let us call in the "technicians," who will give us an "objective" answer unstained by the dark prejudices of choice, taste, bias, and passion. In other words, they will tell us how to maximize our psyches, we shall believe and accept and follow. Result: Our politicians have depoliticized politics as neatly as the Utilitarians and the economists.

The grotesque results of these beautifully harmonious theories are all about us. Are there too many unemployed for our taste? Solution: Delete from the figures those who have tired of looking for work and have dropped out of the "job market." Does the law of supply and demand work for Consolidated Edison of New York? Hardly. When pleas to reduce the use of electricity were met with a marked drop in consumption, Con Edison petitioned for and was awarded a rate increase on the grounds that it was selling less, and thus had to charge more for each unit. Does the "law" of supply and demand work for any other mammoth company, whether a public utility monopoly or not? The answer must be that the "law" functions so grossly that millions of people are cast into poverty, some for many years, before "balance" reasserts itself—if it ever does. The Constitution tell us that we may not be deprived of our property without due process of law. But what legal process has been invoked in the destruction of our savings brought on by long-standing chronic inflation? A massive process of redistribution is taking place, with most victims utterly helpless to protect themselves.

Example can be piled on example of the effects of the mechanistic and egoistic construction of the world which has seized on our minds. They come down to a world view which can be summarized thusly:

· Social life is a "system."

· An inherent "purpose" of all "systems" is to maintain themselves. (I put those words in quotation marks because I find it revolting to impute "purpose" and thus a kind of life to "systems." Even though these ideas are not mine, I have emotional trouble even in expressing them.)

· System-maintenance, so far as the system is concerned, is "good."

· Systems change to avoid breakdown (read "pain") and achieve continuity (read "pleasure").

· This homeostatic, or self-adjusting, quality of "systems" every now and then demands human intervention, just as sometimes a computer program needs to be overridden to take care of special cases. Any intervention implies danger, whether in computers or social "systems," because only system-threatening instability requires such action. The role of political men is to accomplish those interventions. Thus, they are "crisis managers," whose purpose is to reestablish self-governing equilibrium.

· Ergo, the "good system" (the one running along most automatically under its own steam) is one that needs the least politics.

And so, in an updated modern way, this world view reaffirms the basic conclusion of the Utilitarians: society is no more than the sum of agglutinated individual and equal sets of psychologically imputed desires; the more that social life directly permits the unsullied expression of that natural psychological, individual phenomenon, the better; thus, the less politics the better.

While there is little doubt that a self-regulating economic structure was seen as self-evidently good by our Founding Fathers, they also understood that structured political activity was a necessary, desirable, and unavoidable part of life and of the defense of economic rationality itself. The pretense that the best politics is the least politics is a highly ideological and politicized Utilitarian posture. The related assumption, that particular historical problems can be solved by the technical application of universal social "laws," is an equally highly charged political bias, not least because it expels from the process of decision making people who would posit opposing ideas.

The Utilitarian world view has gone so far that it is now in direct clash with the spirit as well as the structural prescriptions of the Constitution. Evidence for that statement seeps from all aspects and levels of American political life. The assumption of ultimate policy leadership by the executive branch of the federal government, for example, is justified by the argument that social affairs have become too complex, too dependent on rapid data accumulation and analysis, to be entrusted to the clumsy mechanism of a legislature; and the defalcation by Congress of its policymaking role has been excused on similar grounds. This is a direct consequence of a failure to think in the straightforward terms of politics—power, interests, ideological preferences, the weighing off of national as against local concerns—and a failure to maintain the general ethical and institutional dimensions within which technicians would be given legitimate room to be apolitical in the narrow and confined sense. Given this disturbance in executive-legislative relations, the court system has moved in and become a partial surrogate for Congress, forced (often against its partisan and jurisprudential will) to give Constitutional mandate *policy* primacy over the great inertia of our mechanistic world view. For that reason the "separate but equal" postulate that arose during the tag end of the last century has given way, and we have reverted to the original Constitutional idea that in political affairs to be separated is *prima facie* to be made unequal. The "one-man-one-vote" dictum is another example of the courts' implementing the basic intention of the Constitution: that equality refers primarily to equality of *condition,* and then, in second place, to equality in opportunities to utilize or spring forth from that basically equal political state.

The courts have long attempted to nurture the doctrine that ultimate political preference should be lodged with Congress and not passed into the hands of technocratic alienators. The basic rule of the game, as the courts defined it in uncomplicated interpretation of the Constitution, is that *the executive branch may administer no policies whose bounds are not previously established by legislative action.* A long parade of cases referring to everything from oil policy and arms sales to the vending of kosher chickens attests to the court's stubborn attachment to the structural requirements laid down by the Constitution. The persistence of the issue testifies equally, however, to a tidal wave of technicism and scientism which seeks to impose a managerial-technocratic, authoritarian "meritocracy," offering as bait the easy idea that government should be but an automatic shift, linking the spinning of egoistic psyches to the satisfaction of their desires.

The *laissez-faire* of the Enlightenment referred to allowing persons to reason within proper institutional orders. Today's derivative *laissez-faire* seeks to allow appetite to work its will, with reason reduced to a supporting role as occasional interventor when the machine breaks down. While both schools of thought separate will from mind, Liberalism sought a reconciliation, while Utilitarianism subordinates the intellect.

There is decreasing room for play between the Liberal inspiration of the Constitution and the Utilitarian inspiration of most politicians, scholars, and businessmen. The reason is not only that the tension constantly makes for grotesque attempts at reconciling practice with mandated organization, attempts that are bound to end in falsehood and self-deception, but, worse, that the strain has caused our systems of accountability to break down. The state and its bureaucracy find difficulty in controlling themselves, let alone in guiding our political affairs. The mix of monopoly, internationalism, and competitiveness in the economy makes the dream of "fine-tuning" impossible, for the market now encapsulates qualitatively different kinds of economic agencies and actors. The political parties are numb and unresponsive, and citizens of all persuasions are beat about by forces they can neither understand nor control. Such is the effect of assuming that ideologies are evil, that politics is an activity to be avoided, that the mind has no control over the gut. Indeed, the entire distinction between mind and will may be a destructive delusion.

If development implies an increasing ability to control physical and social environments as well as oneself, then a loss of institutional accountability implies that the country is "disdeveloping." Concomitantly, the erosion of structures that force accountability on public institutions (which is the Constitution's major point and purpose) necessarily implies that political activity can no longer help us to be effective in submitting our destiny to intellectually disciplined choices—choices which should be argued through and tentatively accepted in order to create a public will to concerted action. The mechanics are destroying our legal and structural foundations, our ability to reason, and what remains of our limited power to make our own lives. That outcome should logically have been expected of the antihistorical, anti-institutional bias of the Utilitarians. However, even though the Utilitarian is in direct ethical opposition to the historically rooted, institutionalist, rationalist persuasion of the Republic's founders, the disease was born with them.

Class and Nation Senator Edward Kennedy has said that the writers of the Constitution caused ". . . a wicked tragedy. They failed to deal with racial equality, and eighty-five years later there was civil war, and we bleed now in Boston. . . ." [7] It was not only racial inequality with which the Constitution failed to deal; the inequalities perpetuated by social class remain similarly unresolved. This flaw pierces the heart of the Constitution, and was from the beginning a threat to the very political community the founders thought they were establishing.

The contradiction between equal membership in a political community and unequal privilege and deprivation in a social community was evident when the Constitution was ratified. Much of the controversy over acceptance of the document raged between affluent lawmakers and less socially favored Americans who feared that an internal colonialism would be imposed in place of the British parent plant. And behind the colonists' formal debates were the cautious (but not totally comprehending) words of the contract theorists, who knew perfectly well that no contract could equally bind slave and free man, uncontrolled rich and servile poor. Rousseau sarcastically expressed the argument made by the favored that lower orders willingly enter into political community with them: "You need me, for I am rich and you are poor. Let us therefore make a contract with one another. I will do you the honor to permit you to serve me under the condition that you give me what little you still have left for the trouble I shall take in commanding you." [8]

Understanding of this contradiction pervaded the political thought of the nineenth century, too. Utilitarians, Social Darwinists, and others thought to sweep the issue under the rug by talking only about individuals and never about community itself. Marxists went the other way, making the contradiction between particular and universal interest the polemical as well as theoretical cornerstone of a general social theory of capitalist society. " . . . Marx contends that in modern society man is cut into two distinct persons—into the 'citizen' (*citoyen*) and the 'bourgeois.' Within the state man is expected to live up to universal criteria; within civil society he is supposed to behave according to his egotistical needs and interests." [9] This fracturing of behavior and standards of comportment leads to the false belief that the state does, indeed, speak in the name of all citizens, when in truth it is but responding to the unequal distributions of power in "civil society." The result, of course, is that men betray their own interests by lending their consent to an instrument of their own oppression. Whether or not one agrees with Marx's construction of the case, he and his followers at least understand the unrealized ideal of Liberalism—the community of universal membership—and applaud its ambition, if not its perverse reality.

The stress between being citizen and being class member of a *bourgeoisie* was recognized by more than Marxists. Max Stirner, using the same categories, came to a conclusion opposite to that of Marx: [10]

Not individual man—and it is only as such that man exists as a real person—has been emancipated [by the French Revolution]; it is merely the citizen, the *citoyen,* political man, that has been liberated; and he is not real man, but just an exemplar of the human species, to be more precise, of the genus *citoyen.* It is only as such, and not as man, that he has been liberated . . . In the French Revolution it is not the individual that is world-historically active: only the nation.

The universal political community was denied importance by the Utilitarians, honored as an admirable but betrayed ideal by the Marxists, deemed the destruction of individual freedom by Stirner's followers, and sanctified by the Hegelians to the point that persons were deprived of importance. For Hegel and his followers, the grinding of the dialectic permitted one to evoke the spirit of the people as a totality, a culture. So, the Hegelians resolved the person-community relational dilemma by erasing the social meaning of the person. No contemporary social theory has as yet gone beyond one of these four positions. We may be in post-industrial society, but we are certainly as yet not in post-nineteenth-century intellectual life. The issue now demands some practical resolution, however, for the failure of the state to represent the nation has cast us into a crisis of loyalties, and thus of legitimacy, which threatens to destroy the regularity of daily social life. The disaffection involves not only "underclasses"; elites and sub-elites—to use nonclass terms—also no longer know to what to be faithful, to what to be loyal, to what to give legitimacy and consensual acceptance. The confusion is so great that even political leaders are in combat as to what it is that they, in turn, are supposed to be loyal. To their immediate constituencies? To some idea of the national interest? To regional prejudices? To law as applied by the courts? To ideological beliefs concerning absolute right and wrong? This destruction of a sense of loyalty, and with it the mechanics of and criteria for accountability, is a direct result of that "wicked tragedy," that unwillingness to establish social equality as the precondition for the promotion of positively useful personal difference. The flaw of the constitutionalists was that they fudged this priority, instead permitting the idea to develop that equality and difference are on the same level, of the same order of political importance and generality.

A rejection of the bedrock importance of community characterizes the Utilitarian reading of the Constitution. The case is bluntly put in a Supreme Court decision of 1915, concerning the right of an employer not to hire a unionized switchman.[11] The majority opinion reads, in part:

. . . since it is self-evident that, unless all things are held in common, some persons must have more property than others, it is from the nature of things impossible to uphold freedom of contract and the right of private property without at the same time recognizing as legitimate those inequalities of fortune that are the necessary result of the exercise of those rights. But the Fourteenth Amendment, in declaring that a State shall not 'deprive any person of life, liberty or property without due process of law,' gives to each of these an equal sanction; it recognizes 'liberty' and 'property' as co-existent human rights, and debars the States from any unwarranted interference with either. . . .

The dissenting opinion, written by Justice Holmes, argued that equality of condition was necessary before a valid contract could be entered into. Labor organization creates that parity of power between employer and employees necessary to the *sense* of the freedom to enter into compacts. Specifically:

". . . In present conditions a workman not unnaturally may believe that only by belonging to a union can he secure a contract that will be fair to him. . . . If that belief, whether right or wrong, may be held by a reasonable man, it seems to me that it may be enforced by law in order to establish the equality of position between the parties in which liberty of contract begins."

In the disagreement of the Justices the problem is crystallized: if the labor theory of value is not accepted, then "life," "liberty," and "property" become separate, "co-existent human rights"—not joined evocations of a single fact, human activity. If they are shredded, deprived of their common root, then equality of social condition becomes impossible: "property" is made equal in weight to "liberty," and the protection of one can signal the diminution of the other. In effect, liberty becomes, like property, a commodity whose distribution is subject to social disputation. Agreements—contracts—about life and work and property will then, necessarily, be entered into unequally. And thus, even the contract theories of the classical Liberals go by the board. But such a destruction of the Constitution's historical sense carries away with it the only reason to ask loyalty of the citizenry. To withdraw loyalty invites repression, the destruction of liberty. The consequence of an unequal distribution of liberty to engage in equal and equally effective action within the community must ultimately lead to the destruction of community itself. The founding fathers lived in an age that believed in the so-called contract theory; indeed, they wrote a document they thought of as a compact, or contract. One of the major and continuing positive myths of the American system concerns the sanctity of contract—an agreement *freely* entered into, with clean hands, by *equals* for the establishment of a set of mutual obligations, and presumably for the mutual benefit of the contracting parties. A parity of duties and benefits is implicit to the idea of contract, and such parity cannot result if the contracting parties are substantively unequal in their ability to enter into a compact.

The maintenance of slavery and class privilege does more than merely deny the benefits which men such as Adam Smith had suggested would flow from the interaction of men equal before the economic order. It also voids the sense of contract, because it denies parity, demanding of some people duties and sacrifices which are of a different order and nature from the reciprocal duties and sacrifices it is willing in turn to extend to them. To be explicit, a national community asks of its citizens that they be prepared to die in its defense and to accept its laws as absolute. Or, putting it another way, the American government asks of *all* of us that we be willing to give it our lives (our physical beings) and our obedience (our belief-system). But it does not ask these sacrifices of the personal to the general will equally, nor does it offer something equally precious in exchange—that is, it does not obey the fundamental prescriptions of equity and equality involved in contract. To wit:

1. It asks blacks much more than whites to die in battle.

2. By and large, it asks the poor to hurt more in paying for the state than the rich.

3. It punishes the crimes of the poor more than it does white-collar crime.

4. It demands greater adherence to the law by political dissidents than by those who politically agree with the powers-that-be.

5. It expects loyalty to the formal state, but not loyalty to the nation.

6. It returns little loyalty to citizens and none to some, even betraying Americans of dissident political belief to the officials of foreign countries.

In short, the state is acting in its own interest and in that of certain privileged groups, and not in the interest of the social nation. Even worse, it denies to *all*—rich and poor alike—that one social duty or obligation which would honor the "contract" by being equivalent to the physical and moral sacrifices made by its people. What is this absolute obligation of the state which has not been delivered? Again we must return to the Enlightenment, and especially to Rousseau, who first saw with stark clarity and *mutual* obligations involved in the creation of a true nation-state, a society of genuinely universal participation:

To him [Rousseau] freedom did not mean arbitrariness but the overcoming and elimination of all arbitrariness, the submission to a strict and inviolable law *which the individual erects over himself. . . .* [italics added] Here lies the heart of the whole political and social problem. It is not a question of emancipating and liberating the individual in the sense of releasing him from the form and order of the community; it is, rather, a question of finding the kind of community that will protect every individual with the whole concerted power of the political organization, so that the individual in uniting himself with all others nevertheless obeys only himself in this act of union. "Each man, by giving himself to all, gives himself to nobody . . ." [12]

If we are to believe in a social compact, what, then, is it which the state must give as its *quid pro quo* in the contractual relation which demands of the citizen possibly his life, and always the submergence of his particular will to the general will in social matters? The only apposite obligation, the only parity of duty, is that the state must provide absolute protection of the citizen, and absolute equality before the community, expressing itself through its body of law. Again Cassirer on Rousseau is absolutely clear on this score:

". . . Common dependence on the law is . . . the only legal ground for any social dependency whatever. A political community that demands any other kind of obedience is internally unsound. Freedom is destroyed when the community is asked to subject itself to the will of a single man or to a ruling group which can never be more than an association of individuals. The only "legitimate" authority is that authority which the principle of legitimacy, *the idea of law as such,* exercises over individual wills. At all times, this idea claims the individual only insofar as he is a member of the community, an actively participating organ of the general will, but not in his particular existence and individuality. No special privilege can be granted to an individual as individual or to a special class; no special effort can be demanded of him. In this sense the law must act "without respect of persons." A bond that does not bind absolutely everyone, but only this man or that, automatically nullifies itself . . . every exceptional decree to which single citizens or certain classes are subjected means by its very nature the destruction of the idea of law and of the state: the dissolution of the social contract and the relapse into the state of nature, which is characterized in this connection as a pure state of violence.[13]

The raw absoluteness of Rousseau's position, the uncompromising insistence on the mutuality of obligation, has often been misread. Some see only the side of him which insists on absolute obedience to law and call him a totalitarian. Others call him unrealistic and inconsistent when they read his statements that he is uninterested *per se* in whether persons are poor or rich, but only in whether poverty or wealth affects the application of the laws. The intricacies of the theoretical argument need not concern us: what *is* important is that many of the citizen's obligations about which Rousseau wrote are still considered to be part of our conventional public morality. It could not be otherwise, for Rousseau is the ultimate theorist of the nation-state, of nationalism, and of the national community. And we Americans have always prided ourselves on being the first new nation, a land of patriots, exemplars of the rule of law. Thus, contemporary examples of Rousseau's evocation of responsibility abound:

· We pride ourselves that people present themselves to draft boards, beginning a process that might end in their deaths, merely upon receipt of a letter requesting their appearance.

· The entire system of income taxation we employ is predicated upon honesty and willing acceptance of the obligation of payment.

· In the 1960s, in the age of burned draft cards and the like, many people simultaneously defended illegal actions for moral purposes and the requirement that such lawbreaking be legally sanctioned. In both violating and sustaining law, they sought morality in a specific act and in the general maintenance of a lawful society.

· Until very recently, it used to be a source of great pride that the United States didn't break treaties—like those untrustworthy foreigners.

These myths are of the essence of national community. Upon their integrity rests the system of interacting loyalties that can bind together over 200 million persons, making them identify certain of their interests as held in common. That interest is no less than maintenance of the national community, permitting the development of individual skills which can be hooked together to create the material as well as political power of the nation.

Now the essential problem can be simply put. It is as follows:

· Our laws demand *absolute* obedience at any given time to extant law, in the presumption that the law itself is temporary and can be changed in accordance with prescribed procedure ultimately involving the participation of all the citizenry.

· The *practical* reason for accepting that relation between the absoluteness of action in a given moment and its relativeness through time is that it sustains the political community, the nation, giving it viability at any given moment and yet flexibility through time.

· The *ethical* justification for accepting the temporal absoluteness of law is that freedom can be attained only through such acceptance. That is, absolute cession of will concerning community thereafter opens up freedom for the individual.

· That freedom has lasting strength only if *all* are equally constrained, equally benefited, equally judged, so that persons do not lend their wills to any other person or group, but to the totality.

· The cession of will is to the community, the nation. The making of law involves the state and the polity—the government and its ancillary political agencies, such as parties and pressure groups. The administration of the laws takes place only through the formal institution of the state, the government.

· Among the nation and the state and government, the structured inequalities of class and race enter to pervert equality in the demands made of citizens and in the guarantees to them. The state and government, instead of speaking and acting in the name of the total political community, become agents of special groups and sometimes even only of special individuals. Eventually the government may become a bureaucratic interest unto itself and speak only in its own name.

· Such a breakdown in the parity of duties and privileges is an ethical violation of the social contract, and so voids it. When enough people become aware of the disparities between demands and recompense, the "social contract" in its nontheoretical mundane sense also breaks down. That is, consensus and legitimacy go by the board, law and lawmakers and law enforcers are mocked, and the community loses its power. With a loss of power goes also a failure of the ability to force social instrumentalities to submit themselves to control. The country becomes anarchic.

Such is our present situation. The matter has gone so far that it is becoming difficult for many persons even to know when they are being loyal or disloyal. That situation evidently describes industrialists involved with global corporations. Can they reconcile their "loyalty" to foreign stockholders with their loyalty to fellow American citizens? The same is true of policemen. Should they denounce fellow Americans as "leftists" to the cops of foreign countries? The same is true of unemployed black youths. Should they be more loyal than others and join the army in order to make a living, and thus increase their chances of being killed in battle?

The national interest is not difficult to discern. It lies not in this specific policy or in that ideological line or in the other special arrangement. It lies in a responsible community of universal membership, with equal obligations and equal rights to protection and adjudication of interests. Any other politics is one of special interest, not of national interest. Any other politics destroys the maturation of differences among persons.

THE
LONE EAGLE

ABROAD

hat's wrong with America has not to do with blind forces, fate, or human nature. It was not Ms. Clio who despatched bombers to celebrate Christmas. It was not Mr. Kismet who plotted ways to "waste" foreign leaders. It was not Sheik Invisible Hand who raised the price of petroleum. It was not General Survival who sent Russians into Hungary and Americans into the Dominican Republic. No, no—the primary responsibility for our conditions rests with our leaders and those who immediately surround and support them. Secondarily, of course, the middling comfortable do share the guilt, for it is power derived from their consent which leaders employ. Still, we should not wash away the difference between using overt power to issue an order and permitting a general situation to exist by tacit consent.

That America's leaders have chosen a technocratic and interest-bound path is obvious. But there would be no contradiction in the situation, nothing to talk about or to make politics about, if the choices they made were the only ones that American society would have permitted. No painstaking analysis of social-science data is needed to accept the assertion that other ways and means could have been chosen. If all Americans were in ideological agreement with their leaders, there would have been no outcry over government corruption, dishonesty, persecution, misuse of police powers, invasion of privacy, murder plots, or the other niceties which have recently been exposed to them. Would Americans be sane if they approved of inflation and depression? Are student dissidence, race riots, and antibussing demonstrations signs of approval? Do extraordinarily low voter turnouts signal satisfaction with the system or, instead, a belief that our political parties and their nominees are empty of significance for what bothers us?

The contradictions between Liberalism and Utilitarianism, and between nation and class, are made real precisely by this discord. It is not that the leadership wants one set of choices, the general public another. Instead, the public is divided and ambivalent, and unable to choose. Its helplessness is due to its lacking effective means of selecting from among alternatives openly explained and debated. And here the reason is that almost all of our elites—politicians, intellectuals, businessmen, journalists—seem able to think only in mechanistic and stale acceptance of the *status quo,* or its mild amendment. Public dissatisfaction thus takes the form of intellectual milling, a generalized restlessness whose fluidity suggests alarming possibilities.

Foreigners show their ignorance of the American scene when they accuse this country of naivete because of its shock and outrage at political scandals. Americans almost universally do agree that governments tend to degeneration; that is the reason the Constitution seeks to cage politicians. The shock and outrage reflect not ingenuousness, but an awareness that we have been fooled, that our institutions have become poor agencies for control, and that consent given for one set of purposes has been twisted back upon itself to create a counterfeit consensus, a formalistic electoral approval of the acts of those who tell us they know better than we.

A Spanish proverb has it that every people has the government it deserves. This adage does not fit the American case.

The public's agony about the distance between the real and the ideal is not mirrored in government policy, although many public officials have also become queasy about the effects of their policies. The general solidity and consistency of governmental prejudices, nevertheless, show most starkly in foreign policy, where the executive branch is given freest rein to reveal itself, to demonstrate clearly what it thinks reality and human nature to be. In acting on foreign peoples, and particularly on weak ones, our elite displays itself in the nude, draped only in wisps of Congressional restraint. In no other area can we more surely assign responsibility. The actors are known, their errors and defeats are notorious, and the ignorance in which they have for so long kept their fellow citizens is now undeniable.

Examining American behavior overseas, moreover, can teach us whether the patterns of our own domestic problems appear in other national situations. The American Revolution was not an isolated phenomenon. One should expect that some of the ideas and structures molding our lives must also have influenced others in the West European cultural continuum. After all, special constructions of arguments about community, public and private interest, and man's place in the universe are endemic to all countries touched by the capitalistic, democratic, secular brush.

Let us, then, turn to international relations for two purposes: to reveal American leadership as it behaves when untrammeled by domestic rules; and to see what it does in specific cases to weak countries attempting to solve problems which are variants of our own. This exploration will lead us to an understanding of why American foreign policy has so consistently, unhesitatingly, and stubbornly supported repressive regimes throughout the world.

Bipartisanship and Other Myths[1] Since the 1930s American foreign policy has been intellectually divorced from domestic politics on the ground that the former involves a *status* (security) on which all parties can agree, and the latter a process (the distribution of values) concerning which legitimately expressed disagreement is the motor force of politics. Bipartisanship can be a legitimate approach to foreign relations if there is no argument over the national interest. Because our foreign policy has reflected special interest, and not the promotion abroad of the welfare of our entire community, bipartisanship has had to be made an extreme appeal. Physical survival—the crudest, most animallike argument—was used to sell bipartisanship as a self-evident good. Consequently, every foreign hassle we have gotten into has had to be defined as a threat to our very lives. But it is not easy to persuade anybody that three million underdeveloped Guatemalans, half of them Indians, could destroy us as a nation. Or that the Dominican Republic or Vietnam, or any of the many other places we have ravaged from the Congo to Cambodia, were live, immediate threats to our land. Two key arguments were used to justify what otherwise would appear merely silly. One was the idea of a universal, monolithic Communist conspiracy dedicated single-mindedly to the destruction of America and the remainder of the "free" world. The other was the domino theory—let us lose but once and the other pieces will topple until we are fighting in the streets of San Diego or Miami.

Many dangers lurk in these arguments. The first is, of course, that they are almost entirely wrong—but just a little bit correct. That is, there can be no doubt that certain Communist countries, particularly the Soviet Union, do indeed threaten the total integrity of the nation. But bellowing wolf over Chile and Laos blunts the poignancy of the cry when a truly vital area is in play. Another danger is that the purveyors of this monolith-domino story are not complete hypocrites: they believe what they are saying. But their misdiagnosis for the American public threatens only democracy; their misdiagnosis for themselves threatens the world, since they control the weapons of total destruction. A third danger of bipartisanship and its supporting rationale is that it weakens domestic social organization, sacrificing the real national interests of some groups to the equally real international interests of others. This straining of the fabric of loyalty and democratic interaction is evidence in and of itself that foreign policy is just another arena in which we bark at each other; it is not a truly bipartisan affair, but only yet another way of mustering uninformed, ignorant agreement.

International politics now involves as many ethical, ideological, and moral determinations affecting national interests as does domestic politics. The wars of nation-states have long since caught up total populations, with correspondingly growing costs and more and more intimate effects on the creation, uses, and distribution of material benefits at home. Now the international economy is also growing in its ability to affect power distributions within developed as well as developing states. The best-known instruments here are the transnational corporations and their allies in spirit, the governmentally dominated international cartels. With equally sprightly maneuvers, both manipulate prices so as to destroy any reasonable relation between cost of production and ultimate market price. The transnationals do so by taking advantage of differing labor and other costs in the many countries they operate in. The government cartels do so simply by wielding the power inherent in monopoly. The often abrupt redistributions of wealth imposed by the cartels, together with the cheap labor tactics of the private companies, first affect already vulnerable social elements in industrialized as well as in developing countries. The most obvious result is that the trade union structure is weakened almost everywhere. If this attack on unions were the only effect of the new trends, that alone would be enough to suggest that the power constellation within the United States is being changed from the outside in a process as yet beyond the control of domestic political decisions.

But cartels and transnationals are not the only new elements on the international scene. Politically organized international economic structures such as common markets and customs unions may also help to destabilize systems of internal power allocations. Even though the major difference between national and international politics is that the latter lacks any body of law stemming from social and political community, in both arenas the same problem is being played out—the grounds on which present individual and group privilege will be maintained or transformed.

America's many international defeats and domestic difficulties have eroded the government's ability to continue with its international adventurism. But a quiet shelving of the old rhetoric still leaves us with the old ideas which have supported the now anachronistic language. Those ideas are no better than the propaganda that once was used to justify them. Let us look at three of them—examples of how the tactics, strategies, and rhetoric of a bipartisan Cold War continue to prevent clean thought.

The first pervasive fallacy is the argument that what we have been doing in and to the world in recent years is "internationalism" and that its opponents are "new isolationists." This balderdash is Orwellian newspeak, for it labels as internationalists those who believe in *Festung Amerika,* in unilateral weight-throwing overseas, and calls isolationist the opposite belief in multilateral cooperation with foreign states. Let us not forget that most of the isolationists of the 1930s favor recent American foreign policy. But those who oppose it, many of them classical "internationalists," do so not because they think the United States should and can live alone, but precisely because they are convinced that it cannot. What is at issue is not isolationism versus internationalism; everyone knows we are a world power and will remain so, even in a time of shifting power ratios. The issue is *how* the United States should act in international affairs, not *whether* it should. The pseudo-internationalists of recent years have built entangling alliances for other nations while retaining America's unitary criteria of action (incidentally violating many treaties along the way, especially in Latin America, with our promises of nonintervention in the internal affairs of other nations). They do not accept the mutuality of obligation, and they compromise only with the greatest reluctance. They have no desire to establish a community of interests involving the happiness of nations living and sharing together. The readiness to act in truly multilateral fashion requires an attempt to create interests whose sharing might generate a complex, broad basis for international comity, in much the same way as one seeks to create a national community within one's own borders. The logic of the world crisis invites us to this stance of genuine international sociability, but our country is ill-prepared to think in the generous terms the situation demands.

A second fallacy is that our actions have been and are "practical," the product of value-free "pragmatism." Here the error lies in the application of Utilitarianism to international relations, a Utilitarianism specifically dressed up for contemporary use in the 1950s by the complacent "celebration of America"—the idea that we had solved our basic organizational problems and needed only to continue to administer into being for others the better world we had already entered. The presumption that there remain no overarching questions about our total "system" is now clearly exposed as wrong. But it had for long been patently false for the entire developing world, where the fundamental issue is precisely what shall the whole national society be. So, while developing countries were concerned with fundamental matters of policy and substance, we insisted on selling them "technical" solutions and rejected any discussion of what we were being "technical" about. There are no technical solutions to basic policy questions. Bertrand Russell put the matter more elegantly:

The power conferred by technique is social, not individual. . . . Scientific technique requires the co-operation of a large number of individuals organized under a single direction. Its tendency, therefore, is against anarchism and even individualism, since it demands a well-knit social structure. Unlike religion, it is ethically neutral, it assures men that they can perform wonders, but does not tell them what wonders to perform. In this way, it is incomplete. . . . The men at the head of the vast organizations which it necessitates can, within reason, turn it this way or that as they please. The power impulse thus has a scope which it never had before. The philosophies that have been inspired by scientific *technique* are power philosophies, and tend to regard everything non-human as mere raw material. Ends are no longer considered; only the skillfulness of a process is valued. This . . . is a form of madness. It is, in our day, the most dangerous form.[2]

The results of this madness are scattered about the world for all to see. Technicians have designed educational programs based on estimates of manpower "needs" which literally have nothing to do with what has actually happened. Attempts to control monetary inflations in country after country have led both to continued inflation and the onset of economic depression. "Successful" industrialization programs leave blue-collar workers more impoverished than when they began and economic elites much better off—a result that invites political repression. Revolutions do not occur where predicted, and do occur where not predicted.

The ultimate sadness is that domestic disarray in the United States, added to our technocratic approach to the rest of the world, have destroyed the appeal of this country as a model for democratic development. It is no solace that the Soviet Union has suffered an equal loss of attractiveness. What is left are some vague impressions about mainland China and some half-baked ideas about the use of one or another pattern of military force. But the major guiding visions of the past are gone, victims of the massed force of the nibblings of innumerable small minds.

Bipartisanship, together with technocratic programs and policies effected in isolation overseas, invites a third and crowning fallacy: that we can promote national community by being antinational. This inversion of reason is as common here as in most of the Third World, especially in Latin America. In brief, people who wrap themselves in the flag and proclaim the sanctity of the nation are usually racists, contemptuous of the poor, and dedicated to keeping the community of "ins" small and pure of blood, spirit, and mind. People who have compassion for the poor and like to think about embracing all their fellow citizens are too often ashamed to use the symbols of nationhood. Thus, we are left with antinational nationalists and national antinationalists. That America's leadership falls into the first category, both at home and abroad, is all too plain. Overseas the complications arising from this position can be devastating, for to stand against the passion of a true nation pulling itself into being requires more force than we are usually prepared to apply. Vietnam is a case in point. So is Cuba.

Because democratic nation-building has been rendered impossible by the recent foreign policies of the United States as well as of many European states, true nation-building has usually been undertaken under some kind of leftist political banner. Any such left-leaning tendency in establishing the patterns of a total community, in imposing goals on technical prowess, and in forcing the United States to understand and adjust inevitably unleashes the howling witches. Dominoes click, monoliths swell, and the vitals tremble. Retribution can be expected. But if a country decides to be "sensible," to recognize the eternal verities of hierarchy and mechanistic economics, to leave ethics for the future and clutch to momentary survival, then it can be friends with America—even if it decides that a little torture is a necessary part of "development."

This is no exaggeration. It is many years since we have effectively attempted to help a developing country that has tried to build a truly national community on the basis of which democracy might have room to develop. But we daily help terrorists and murderers, long after even our allies have become sickened—as by the Greek and Chilean juntas. Perhaps our leaders have decided that the world is fatally bipolar—it must be either capitalistic or communistic; and if capitalism must be supported by terror, then so be it—at least it is our kind of horror. If that, indeed, is their view of our situation, then they have made a choice not merely for others but for ourselves, should our present crises continue to deepen.

If our options are seen so narrowly by our guiding elites, then indeed the danger is great. Even though the world is by no means that simple, nor the alternatives logically cast in that way, our elites at least temporarily have the power to enforce their purblind vision. Two Latin American cases, almost pure examples of our own class-nation schism, will be sufficient to exemplify the distortion. The Cuban government has elected to attempt to destroy class and build an absolutely all-inclusive national community. The Chilean government has elected to destroy the nation and erect an iron structure of class privilege. Neither, of course, is democratic. Why have we harassed Cuba, to the point of embarrassment? Why do we support Chile, equally to the point of embarrassment? I have given intellectualized answers above; now let us attend to the cases themselves.

Cuba The histories of Cuba and the United States have been intimately tied for well over a century. The links have to do not only with the well-known facts of political history—the Maine, Theodore Roosevelt, José Martí, the Platt Amendment, and so on and on through the Bay of Pigs and the Missile Crisis in the early 1960s—the ties are also subtle and intricate, involving a mingling of cultures, certainly in Cuba and evidently in certain cities of this country, too. Cuban exiles have importantly affected political life in the United States through their involvement with intelligence agencies, their effects on national political parties and leaders, and their possible implication in acts of violence far transcending the internecine cannibalism they practice among themselves. But inside the island the pervasive influence of American culture certainly contributed importantly to Cuba's becoming Latin America's first fully participant national society. The presence and the ethos of the Colossus of the North helped to weaken such traditional Hispanic institutions as the Catholic Church, and to convert Cuban farm workers from peons bound to the soil into wage labor—mobile, often unemployed, and thus potentially volatile in their politics. The United States helped to secularize Cuba and give it a relatively advanced capitalistic economy, including the establishment of free labor. These factors assist the building of national community, the truly revolutionary accomplishment of Fidel Castro and his associates.

In this critical organizational endeavor, Castro was squarely in the political tradition of the American Constitution. But, by working the change through socialistic economic devices and by establishing a very particular kind of totalitarian state, he just as squarely was pushed out of the tradition. But when Castro was just a radical nationalist, and long before he had hitched himself to the Soviet bloc, the enmity of the United States had become absolute. Casting aside formal treaty obligations, solemn pledges, and the sense of our membership in both the United Nations and the Organization of American States, we made mini-war on Cuba and, failing at the Bay of Pigs, blithely continued to support subversion, guerrilla operations, assassination plots, and an entirely illegal blockade and other economic harassment which persist to this day. Certainly only fear of domestic and foreign public reactions prevented American leadership from mounting a full-fledged invasion of the island to back up the failed Bay of Pigs invasion.

America's hostility was justified on the grounds that Castro's Cuba was part of the Communist international apparatus. The depth of the animosity, in turn, made it inevitable that Castro should turn to the Russians, for the matter became literally one of survival for him. Having forced the prophecy to fulfillment, the United States in turn saw its literal physical survival threatened, which is the importance of the Missile Crisis. For the only time in the entire course of the Cold War, the United States and Soviet Union embarked on a confrontation that included, as part of conscious planning, the possibility that the situation would explode into nuclear warfare. The Soviet Union, in placing missiles in Cuba, violated the tacit agreements that had kept East-West tension within bounds. In return for their withdrawal of those weapons, the United States formally agreed not to invade the island. And we returned to an "acceptable" level of odium.

It is not my purpose to describe these events; that has been done often and excellently. The question that interests me is this: What was Cuba doing that our leadership deemed so despicable that we shoved the island into the middle of the Cold War? I suppose the short answer is that they were doing socialism. And at the same time they expropriated about a billion dollars' worth of property owned by American citizens, most of whose value was repaid to the erstwhile owners by the American public. We know the reasoning: If Guatemala had succeeded in "doing it" in the early 1950s, all of Central America would have fallen; and if Cuba had "done it" in the early 1960s, all of Latin America would have followed. One must be neutral about this, and describe what "it" is that Cuba had done by the time that country celebrated the fifteenth year of its revolution.[3]

By the criteria of people interested in standard approaches to economic and social development—agricultural economists, educational specialists, environmentalists, and so forth—Cuba has done spectacularly well. There is no population or urban explosion. Health care is available throughout the island, for all alike, without charge, and of high quality. Preventive medicine has taken great strides. Life expectancy in Cuba is now 71 years for men and almost 74 for women—the highest rate for any Latin American country, and higher than comparable rates for the United States. It would be virtually impossible to create more literates. The number of primary schools and enrolled students doubled in fourteen years. Secondary education is similarly expanding, and the hope is to erase the educational pyramid—to permit Cubans to have some relation to formal schooling throughout their lives. Work and study are combined for all but the youngest students. There is no unemployment, in an island where unemployment used to be chronic and in a region where Jamaica and Puerto Rico, for example, have been running unemployment rates of between 30 and 40 percent. There is little pollution, not least because there are few automobiles. These social gains have been registered despite fiercely hostile external pressures, the need to readjust the entire international market economy of the island, and a series of most serious mistakes in economic planning and management. By the mid-1970s the island was relaxed: the economic picture had evened out, the social gains of the revolution were obvious, international tensions were easing. The foundations for the economic "infrastructure" had been laid; more importantly, the social bases for a society of literate and participant citizens had also been established.

Cuba's political stability is as firm as its currency. Participation in local affairs is extremely widespread, and there is a high level of grass roots democracy, town-meeting style. Good estimates have it that in 1975 there were some 12,000 political prisoners, of approximately 20,000 prisoners for all reasons out of a population of almost 9,000,000. Even though the Cuban definition of a political prisoner is wider than that used in many other countries—in Cuba it includes vagabonds, hooligans, and other such labels common in Communist countries—there is no evidence of torture or other untoward practices, except for the deprivations experienced by those suspected of CIA affiliation. National affairs are decided by a small group at the top of the heap, as are international economic and political policies. Thus, Cuba is authoritarian in the way the nation's posture is set; in the ability of its central government to lay its hands on any individual Cuban, it is totalitarian authoritarianism; and at the local level Cuba is a substantively participant and democratic society.

Cuba's successes are exactly of the kind that our massproduced development experts tell us we should seek. For example, they talk to us of the "Brazilian miracle" because Brazil is ostensibly holding inflation down to 20–30 percent a year, because the foreign exchange picture was good until the international economy was thrown into a spasm by oil prices, because new industries are being built there, and so forth. They hold out for the future an end of illiteracy, improved medical attention, a control of urban expansion—all those things to be done after the economic "base" is built. But Cuba has done these social jobs better than any other Latin country, and is on the way to economic diversification and long-term stabilization. Such feats are really not enough, however, whether in Cuba or Brazil, for they are *quantitative* achievements, not qualitative ones. And, as I shall explain more fully, a quantitative change here does not imply the necessity of another one there, nor does quantity dictate quality. To put it in other terms:

· Participation is not democracy. Nazis mobilized major sectors of the German population, and they participated all too effectively.

· More goods and services do not mean either better goods and services or a better life, once the basic material needs of life are satisfied.

· Egalitarianism is not equity. A repressive state may treat us all unfairly, may equally impoverish our social beings.

· Living in cities or building a city-nation-state as in Cuba, does not create *urbane* persons. Peasants can and do live in great social lumps.

· Indicators of development are not development. The only meaningful measure of development has to do with people, not utility plants, tire factories, and ports.

The Cuban leadership knows all this, but like the rest of us they are not certain how to proceed. Creating the structure of a sovereign nation-state has been their hardwon success; taking the next steps into creative social community will require innovation. In other words, Cuba has entered onto exactly the same problem area as the United States and Western Europe, but with several advantages. The island is small, neat, and easy to administer. Class-nation and race-class-nation stresses have been sharply reduced to shadows of their former importance. And the physical distance from the Soviet bloc and isolation from the United States have served to force Cubans to create a personality of Cubanness. However, difficult impediments lie in the way of Cuba's realizing the freedom and dignity with which its revolution, like all others of its kind and our kind, was justified.

Cuba's problems are intellectually interesting—they should not be thought of in first instance as fuel for partisan snarling. For example, the country is both enjoying and suffering from the fact that it is an open-admissions system. That entire insular world has been opened to the peasantry, the urban blue-collar workers, and the members of the previously stagnant lower white-collar groups. That all these people go to night clubs and cabarets as reward for special effort, or to luxury hotels for their honeymoons, tells only a tiny bit of the story. Their members are recruited to tasks throughout the island, filling not only the posts formerly held by the present refugees, but of course in new positions resulting from the island's social and economic elaboration. Obviously, they cannot come to these new activities with the class-bred finesse of their predecessors. Thus, one finds a certain crudeness, a narrowness of focus—effects of the culture of poverty that was so long a part of the island. The problem is absolutely no different from that of the university system of the City of New York when it embarked on its open-admissions program in the late 1960s. The difficulties have to do not merely with lagging reading skills but with all those elements that go to make up sociability. I am talking of social gracefulness, the forms of courtesy that make impersonal converse easy and pleasant, the containment of everyone's awkwardness and gaucherie by habits of cultivated intercourse among people with a broad range of origins and varied crotchets.

Another Cuban problem has to do with the decay of the cities. Havana is clean but drab. Formerly elegant residential neighborhoods are quite empty of people. The city has lost much of its spark. It's dull. The reasons are complex. Superficial explanations have to do with the newly incorporated people of whom I have just spoken, the absence of automobiles, the massive departure of the upper- and upper-middle-class populations, and so on in that vein. But I suspect the cause lies far deeper, in the very nature of a city that has lost its capitalist functions. Take away the shopping centers, the eating places, the ease of mobility, and the sense of variety which commercial competition has historically brought, and urban style must suffer, together with the decreased ebb and flow of the population. The city is reduced to its classical colonial functions: It becomes a political and bureaucratic center, an educational focus, a transportation hub, and a place to sleep. Theatrical spectaculars may be offered, but where is Off-Off Broadway? Cabarets and nightclubs may flourish, as they do in Havana, but where is that scrabbling, that constant social peristalsis, that rubbing, which permits fad to blend into movement and movement to melt into national style? Wall Street at night suffers from the same emptiness as Havana and Moscow.

A truly urbane city glows with the "positive uses of disorder." It promotes wandering about, the serendipitous emergence of varied ways of looking at the world, or at problems, or at Herblock's cartoons. This variety is of inestimable value in introducing rationality into public matters: it provides the basis of relativism—of anti-absolutism—which is the wellspring of all political morality. Without this purposeful disorder, a city is only a scene in which villagers suffer pollution and crowding.

Socialists, Republicans, technocrats, and red-neck physical planners have trouble thinking about cities. They all put their emphasis on the carrying out of *specific* tasks, so they seek rationalization, the ordering of jobs—but not rationalism, the ordering of priorities, a necessarily relativistic task. Because socialist ideology has gained acceptance in developing countries such as Cuba, much emphasis is understandably placed there on the quantitative developmental task, on discipline in work and social interaction. But to plan only for order and increasing rationalization is to invite merely technical responses to a situation that touches on the core of national life, on its style, tone, feeling, and odor. Cuban urban planners seem very like their counterparts in the United States: Their concerns are quite literally only concrete.

The Cubans have a particular difficulty in thinking about the city. Almost all their revolutionary leaders were born outside of Havana and went to the capital city for their education. They have practiced a revolution based on a rapid underwriting of social change in rural areas and small towns. This process has a fundamental justification: It is a major step in creating a city-nation-state, a totally integrated national society. Thus, the relative physical neglect of Havana and its decline in sociability have been balanced by the educational, health, and organizational integration of all Cubans into participant local communities. This job of physical change is well on its way to completion. Left to be realized is the quality of the achievement; what kind of community have Cubans now joined?

If by socialism we mean more than the nationalization of an economy, then Cuba is not yet a completed socialist state. But a social nation it is, having achieved its French Revolution with staggering thoroughness. And it is not true that the Cuban revolution cannot be rolled back. In the sense that social class may reemerge as a critical social contradiction, the Cubans may yet lose their revolution. Obviously, I am referring to the possible emergence of a bureaucratic authoritarianism, a tropical version of the USSR. The acceptance of a technocratic vision of life, based on a meritocracy, is the great danger facing the libertarian aspirations of many Cubans. The bitter proof of their victory is that they are at the same essential point as is the United States or any other mature Western society. And, like the rest of us, they will have to create new forms and practices if they are to give meaning in daily life to old aspirations.

Chile The murder of Chile's President Salvador Allende on September 11, 1973, shattered into a thousand symbols. The Cuban leadership was not surprised: They had never thought that socialism could flow from the barrels of legislative pens. American leaders were gratified: After all, they had spent many years trying to prevent a leftist coalition from taking power in Chile, and three more years making life generally difficult for Allende. Chilean Christian Democrats and other centrists were overjoyed at the removal of a government they thought illegitimate and threatening to their basic Christian values, and they were hopeful of soon being able to resume political power. Chile's far right continues to rejoice in the end of a government of the Anti-Christ, and remains determined to go on with the totalitarianism they see as natural and fitting to man's nature. The ideologies of Chile's left went mercurially flying. Differing

interpretations continue to grow. The most important understandings are in Europe and the United States, where the Chilean experience lives because it enlightens our own situations.

It speaks well of our troubled minds that the hurts of a small
country of eight million people, perched on a narrow ledge between towering mountains and the blue Pacific, should stick so
in our feelings and our thinking. Lodged in our mental craw is
the fact that Allende's government was legally elected, even
though by a minority of the voters, in a country that had practiced democratic forms for longer than any other Latin American state, and with less violence than the United States. Our actions helped to destroy one of the world's few democracies.
Granted, Chilean democracy had been confined to the favored
classes in society for a century. But by the 1920s formal political
participation was opening broadly to all—and thirty years later
even women were made a part of the national electorate. The
extension of the suffrage long postdated a tradition of press
freedom, openness of political discussion among all social sectors, and a firm history of congressional power unique in Latin
America. In other words, Chile had what is known as a "guided
democracy."

More to the immediate point of the Allende crisis, leftist
movements in Chile had a long, proud, and unique history—
unique in the world, not only in the Americas. Marxism took
root in Chile's labor unions in the early part of this century, and
then slowly spread into an array of political parties, the principal
ones being the usual socialist and communist parties. Most un-
usual, however, was the development of a habit of electoral
combination among those parties of the left. The Chilean Popular Front, for example, was organized in 1936, won the presidency in 1938, and lasted until December 1940 before losing a
socialist faction. This alliance had the longest life of any such
movement in the world. Even after its breakdown, a coalition of
centrist Radicals, Socialists, Communists, and other fragments
of the left held Chile's government until 1947, when the Radicals, the principal party, abandoned the arrangement. Like the
Marxists of France and Italy, Chile's socialist Left has consistently won the allegiance of a third of the population through
many political generations. Allende's victory in 1970 was thus

not a historical shock; the issue for long had been not whether a generally socialist coalition would win, but when.

The appeals that Chile's Left made for social equity were not unfounded. Income and related disparities have been very sharp in Chile, and were made even more acute by the partial industrialization that set in with World War II. It is usual that industrial growth should bring in its train a depression of the real wages of blue-collar workers, leave rural workers in slough, and rapidly increase the advantages of upper-middle- and upper-class persons. This experience, repeated throughout Latin America, is hastened by the chronic relation between inflation and under-employment or unemployment—two ways to ensure profitability. A noted Chilean economist, writing in 1965, said: [4]

The emphasis placed on industrial development has left untouched the traditional system of land-ownership while new forms of high concentration of capital have been created in industry [and other sectors]. . . . As a result income distribution has remained markedly unequal and savings have therefore also tended to be highly concentrated. . . . Because of this high degree of concentration of economic power and the growing association of the higher echelons of the bureaucracy with the industrial and financial groups, the state has increasingly come under the control of private interests. . . .

The increasing imbalance in distribution of income can be appreciated when one finds that the legal minimum wage in Chile declined in purchasing power by more than a third between 1952 and 1970, while the number of persons living at that level increased, their percentage in a growing population remaining about the same during the eighteen years. Farm workers were not permitted to organize into trade unions until 1965, and their minimum wage was set in 1952 for the first time—but at a third of that of urban workers. The expectation, of course, was that those *campesinos* who could do so would eke out their livings by growing subsistence crops for themselves, and by stealing. It is probable that unskilled farm workers suffered a decline of a fifth in their real wages between 1940 and 1952, at a time when salaried employees and owners were enjoying an increase of over 40 percent in the same period. Only after 1964 did real wage rates in agriculture improve measurably, but as late as 1967 nearly 90 percent of rural workers were still earning only the minimum wage, as contrasted to 55 percent of urban workers.[5]

Citation of these grim economic data need not be continued, for they can distort understanding. Chile was a country in which some half of the population lived reasonably well in economic, social, and political terms, and in which the other half fared badly. The two sets of circumstances should be grasped simultaneously in order to understand how it might have been possible to extend social decency to everyone. Chile had the ideological, administrative, governmental, and historical means to attempt to bring all Chileans into a democratic order. That understanding was not restricted to the left; the Christian Democrats were equally persuaded of the possibility and the desirability of completing the social nation. But during their six years in office (1964–1970) they fell far short of their promises— although they by no means betrayed their policy premises. Their problem was in emphasizing economic improvement, and they seriously lagged in creating political ideas and practices to supplement their essentially paternalistic economic programs. Worse, they did not succeed even in maintaining the ideological integrity of their own party, falling into disarray during the 1970 campaign.

The *allendistas* took office in 1970 proposing to maintain and extend the practice of democracy, to be accomplished through a socialization of the economy. They had in their tradition a long practice of coalition politics, attachment to democratic order and party interaction, and respect for constitutional procedure. Given the pressures they had to sustain, they did not do badly in maintaining their historical habits. Much rewriting of Chile's history has taken place since 1973, but let me offer some support for this view from two sources, both of which have tried valiantly to be neutral. One is from a report on Chile prepared by Anmesty International: [6]

Political arrests certainly took place under Allende, both of extreme left and extreme right wing persons. Such political arrests occurred mainly during the periodic states of emergency that were proclaimed throughout the three years of the Allende government. Yet detained persons were released within a few days, on the termination of the State of Emergency. Restrictions were also placed sporadically on the freedom of the press. The leading antigovernment newspaper *El Mercurio* [a longtime recipient of CIA funds, it was subsequently revealed] was closed down for one day in June 1973, after publishing advertisements of the right-wing National Party alleging the illegality of the Allende government. Yet such restrictions were temporary, in contrast to the permanent dissolution since the coup of all newspapers which supported the Allende government.

As for the international subversion that Allende's government was supposed to have supported, here are the conclusions of the Select Committee of the U.S. Senate to study intelligence activities: [7]

. . . the more extreme fears about the effects of Allende's election were ill-founded: there never was a significant threat of a Soviet military presence; the "export" of Allende's revolution was limited, and its value as a model more restricted still; and Allende was little more hospitable to activist exiles from other Latin American countries than his predecessor had been. Nevertheless, those fears, often exaggerated, appear to have activated officials in Washington.

What we have is a small Latin American country whose unique history put it into a position to debate the issue of whether and possibly how to complete its social construction as a nation. Parties of the center and the left agreed on the desirability of meeting this old ideal, but divided sharply on the mechanisms that should be used. Before 1970, however, both center and left agreed that democratic process was to be the *political* means to that end. The center remained committed to mixed economic ways of going about the job, the left to nationalization and socialization. Into this slowly evolving situation stepped the United States, unconcerned about democracy and nation-building, taken up only with the Cold War and dominoes, and all too ready to confuse private ownership with both other issues. The Senate report documents the record of American subversion. Our money bought newspapers (and how we berate others for their corruption!), influenced elections (and how we mock others for faking votes!), plotted coups (and how we do rant about subversives!), and passed weapons to assassins (and how we froth with vengeful frenzy about giving murderers and muggers and dope pushers what they deserve!). And all that was done was without concern for Chile's complexities.

That very complexity implies, of course, that American behavior was therefore only one of many elements in Allende's fall and the emergence of the present situation. Here are the reasons I see for the failure of Allende's attempt at nation-completion, given roughly as I assign them importance:

· Using peaceful and democratic means to work fundamental change in economic structure demands great intelligence and a historical experience on which to draw. No such precedent existed, and Chilean political and social thinkers were not up to the task—whether in theoretical breadth, technical competence, or general intellectual flexibility. Nor was help forthcoming from other sources. Marxist theoreticians from other lands were all too eager to impose their own prefabricated views on Chilean uniqueness. And, needless to say, the world's self-professed democracies were dedicated either to inaction or to subversion, and their social scientists were frozen into immobility.

· The overall political-economic policies of the Allende regime were ill-conceived in that they assumed that their government's power base could not be confirmed without the economic socialism which was their professed goal. Thus, they neglected the political structure which had enabled them to take power in the first place. In other words, they remained captives of economic determinism, belying the politics that had served them so well in giving them their epochal opportunity.

· The government was comprised of an ill-fitting coalition, useful for gaining office but not for consolidating policy. The Socialist Party was generally activist and radical, the Communists cautious and professional and searching for a revival of an alliance with the center, and the Radicals confused and pious. Other splinter groups were equally divided in their approach to the tactical situation.

· The public administration was distributed, within the same ministries, among adherents of the several parties. Thus, coherent policy was difficult to attain even within discrete branches of the public administration.

· The opposition, including the Christian Democrats, started early in the game to become disloyal. They began to play chicken with the government, daring it to violate the sacred constitution, so that the military could be asked to step in. The opposition's disloyalty sealed the fate of a government determined to remain within the broad definitions of democratic practice, as indeed was Allende's dedication—unto his dying moment. It can be said with sadness that, when Allende died, he was perhaps the last man in Chile who still believed in a democratic road to Socialism, "The Chilean Way."

· The disloyalty of the opposition, including the rightist parties as well as the core of the Christian Democrats, spread to the newspapers, the other media of communications, and the trade unions. All too eager to use foreign monies, the opposition created disorder through strikes, false news reports, other forms of economic sabotage, and murder. The CIA had no trouble finding customers for its funds and equipment.

· The "policy of economic denial" embarked on by the Nixon administration removed any room for maneuver as the Chilean government tried to better the conditions of the lowest third of the population while it also aimed for land reform and the nationalization of major industries, banks, and insurance companies. Castro, during his state visit to Chile, remarked caustically that Allende was working a revolution in consumption, while Cuba had attempted to work a revolution in production. The attempts at rapid income redistribution were new for Chile, but the government's heavy involvement in industry and banking was not. Indeed, a mixed economy is what had resulted from the country's thirty-year-old industrial development program.

· The military was an autonomous and thus unaccountable force. It was armed and trained in great part by the United States, and influenced by the "doctrine of internal warfare" developed under the Kennedy administration to legitimate U.S. involvement in foreign civil wars—surrogates for the war with the USSR made highly undesirable by atomic weaponry.

These circumstances dictated Allende's failure, but they do not explain the particular nature of the successor government. Any full explanation must be overly complex for the purposes of this brief survey. Still, it is obvious that a country sophisticated enough to attempt a socialist democratic way of nation-building also has the technical potential for modern totalitarianism. Further, the Chilean population, highly sensitive to political issues, fell easy prey to rumors, inspired fears, hatreds, and class antagonisms that pushed the country into a feral state. Large sections of the middle and upper classes became entirely convinced that not only was their property threatened, but their very lives. Again, American *agents provocateurs* found fertile ground for their activities.

Despite minimal police brutality during the Allende years, despite the repeated attempts of his government to prevent peasant seizures of farms, despite its effective attacks on leftist terror, despite the clear evidence that right-wing murder squads had been operating in the country even before Allende was sworn into office, favored sectors of the Chilean population were entirely convinced that they were now going to be murdered in their beds by rampaging hordes from the slums, or by terrorists working through their execution lists. They are still so convinced, and continue to justify the real terror, death, and torture they helped unleash and still support on this basis of what might have been. There is no arguing the point with them or their North American supporters. The standard legalistic complaint that persons should be judged only on what they have done and not on what they might think, brings only silence. After all, if we were to imprison everyone who has had a criminal thought, only the catatonic and suckling babes would be on the loose. But no matter—the anti-Allende people saw themselves fighting for survival, and they prefer to have killed and to continue killing than to be killed. I find it strange that none of them asks how it was that he was allowed to stay alive long enough to become a killer or the tacit supporter of killers. But then, there is no logic when animal survival becomes the issue.

The military government that assumed power in September 1973, celebrated with a major wave of arrests and summary murders. Nobody knows how many people were killed. Responsible estimates range from 12,000 to 80,000. Since then, summary arrests, torture, disappearances, detentions without trial lasting for years, and other atrocities have been run-of-the-mill occurrences. These findings have been documented by U.S. government officials, in the reports of international commissions both private and public, and the accounts of exiles. Despite world pressure, the practices go on. It is necessary that they do so. The price of promoting class over nation is that the less favored must be taught that they are where they are because they deserve to be there, and any members of the elite who imagine that universal community is a worthy aspiration must learn that the Counter-Reformation did not occur in vain.

Without terror, labor cannot be persuaded to be a commodity—to be quiescent, be unresisting to pressures that cause literal starvation, do its part to make Chile attractive to capital investment. Without terror, the intellectual and professional community cannot be silenced, universities and secondary schools taken over by the armed forces, organs of opinion shut. Without terror, an appearance of "normality" cannot be maintained to permit the comfortable middle class to pretend that the smoke pouring from the chimneys is produced by coal, not flesh. Without terror, the "sanity" of a "rational" marketplace cannot reemerge; and without "sound" market economies, the country will never recover. Without terror, the order which the terrorists helped to destroy cannot be restored.

Again, then, we have lineal, automatic Utilitarian reasoning. The Chilean junta is back to the "trickle-theory" in economics: It will attract investors by keeping the price of labor depressed by force, and economic advance will then permit a little juice to drain down to the parched mouths on the bottom. And the North Americans are in the same logical bag: If they had permitted Allende's democratic socialism to succeed, it would really be Marxist Communism that would have won, leading God knows where. To quote Henry Kissinger: [8]

Now it is fairly easy for one to predict that if Allende wins, there is a good chance that he will establish over a period of years some sort of Communist government. In that case you would have one not on an island off the coast which has not a traditional relationship and impact on Latin America, but in a major Latin American country you would have a Communist government, joining, for example, Argentina, which is already deeply divided, along a long frontier; joining Peru, which has already been heading in directions that have been difficult to deal with, and joining Bolivia, which has also gone in a more leftist, anti–U.S. direction, even without any of these developments.

Thus, the domino theory is used to support preemptive warfare. And in the act of explanation Dr. Kissinger, the grand debater, even suggests that we should not have been so worried about Cuba—"an island off the coast which has not a traditional relationship and impact on Latin America. . . ." Cuba now seems removed from the domino game, a retired piece. He seems unaware that the mistake in reasoning concerning Cuba should alert us to the possibility of a similar error in understanding Chile.

It is indeed rare in human events that two such nearly perfect and perfectly opposing cases should arise in the same cultural area at the same time. The nation-class controversy has played itself out to its limit in each country. We should use the astringency of these ideal types to clean our heads. It should now be apparent that to fall into the simplism of dismissing both Cuba and Chile as totalitarianisms, and therefore the same, is to bar further analysis. The immediate result of Cuba's authoritarianism is a striking increase in the welfare of Cubans—in schooling, health, and many material aspects of life. The immediate result of Chile's authoritarianism is starvation, more illiteracy, and ill health. At least for the time being, Cuba feels open and enthused. Chile feels closed and dank.

But neither situation is desirable for the democratically inclined. To choose class over nation is definitively to close off the possibility of freedom. Chile has doomed itself to continued repression, or to bloody class conflict. There is no possibility of a peaceful transition to equitable, democratic, national community. To choose nation over class, however, makes democracy at least a possibility; it creates a necessary condition, as the scientists say, but not a sufficient condition, for democracy. To get on with the task requires practicing democracy, and keeping down the constant threat of an emerging new class of technocratic bureaucrats. The next years in Cuba will be interesting, although hope must be mixed with fear, given the experiences of the nationalist revolutions in Eastern Europe. As for Chile, the next years can only be grisly, or a little less grisly.

The purity of these two cases has not been lost on Europe's leftists, particularly on Italian Marxists. Their interest in Cuba is marginal, but their concern with the Chilean experience is profound. The reason is obvious: Chile's history speaks to the more advanced situation, to the precious value of even partial democracy, and asks whether it can be maintained and even reinforced during a transition to a more just and politically rewarding economic life. If Americans want to understand the gathering winds of West European politics, reading a good history of Chile would not be an untoward beginning. Allende's vision is alive. Whether his mistakes are dead, however, remains an open question.

As for our own country's policymakers, these two stark cases leave them no shadows to hide in. They sacrificed honor, promises, treaties, honesty, and democracy at home and abroad to stop the building of national communities in these two small countries which, in themselves or even in combination with neighbors, could not have threatened the physical security of the United States. But they certainly did not understand the situation as I have just defined it. Using the domino mentality, equating the particular with the public interest, assuming that the private interest would trickle into the public good, they saw only two Cold War threats—not two places full of Chileans and Cubans, fearing and hoping and exhuding the odors of their own national histories and passions. Our leaders decreased the chance that Cuba can move from nationalism to democracy, erased the hope in Chile, and endangered democratic institutions at home.

Is it possible that the choices they made for Cuba and Chile are the same that they think will have to be made at home? Certainly there must be alternatives other than those symbolized by Cuba and Chile.

THE
ETHIC:
DENIAL AND

AFFIRMATION

he language is pocked with ugly compound words suggesting that the past is gone and the present defies understanding. "Post-industrial," "post-modern," "post-capitalistic," and "post-Marxist" are a few of these monuments to perplexity, to the suspicion that the world is not working the way it is supposed to—or, at any rate, the way it used to. True, the rate of change is speeding up almost everywhere, sweeping ever more people through profound transformations that seem beyond control. But the velocity and extension of change are not at the heart of what is going on, not at the heart of the situation which we have such difficulty in describing. The rapidity of change across whole societies is not even; indeed, the asymmetry of social change is its most striking characteristic. The industrial, scientific, and managerial techniques developed in the past half-century are making it possible to innovate in one set of activities, without having to adjust everything else in narrow, determinate, fixed patterns. In other words, social life is becoming unhinged.

Nothing should be more joyously hailed. Whenever a change here does not necessitate a given change there, then just that much more room for reason and choice is available, that much more grist for the democratic mill. We are gaining the ability not to shake off circumstances, but to control their consequences for the future. Yet fear at the prospect of substituting consciously used reason for custom and habit has struck at the minds of hordes of intellectuals. Many would have us return to the "verities" of the small community, where symmetry and tradition can obviate the painful task of creatively thinking about the construction of the future. But hardly anyone, whether committed to smallness or not, is able to discard an idea which used to be correct—that the spheres of our social activities were bound together in mean and pinched ways allowing little reasoned play. The new technology, belying the old social ways, renders false the predictions as well as the prescriptions of the mentally hidebound. For example, many of America's foreign-policy failures are, at the same time, human successes—evidence that people are becoming highly competent in evading Iron Laws. The almost universal failures of national planning can also be taken to demonstrate that the deterministic premises built into such planning do not describe the realities of social life. Such examples should invite sorrow about our present intellectual condition, but happy excitement when we think what we might make of ourselves.

The most striking example of new possibilities may be found in the fact that the relation between urbanism and urbanity has been broken. That is, the *ecological* position of persons, their physical location, no longer has a determinative bearing on their social empathy, their ability to let their minds roam through historical time and across physical space, soaring beyond the limits of family and tribe. Worldliness is no longer the product only of cities. The importance of this new situation cannot be overestimated; it signals a new age, in which the urban-rural dichotomy declines in favor of a more specific difference among persons: what they are themselves, instead of what they reflect of their geography. A constraint as ancient as history has finally begun to break down.

There are dangers to the change. One is that cities can now

be lived in for long periods of time by villagers. Migrants can be pulled to urban areas from foreign shores or from old-fashioned rural areas and persist in their provincialism. As a result, they do not learn to live in the universalism that cities must have to work—in the affectionate impersonality which permits strangers to live in close cooperation in complex urban settings. Another danger is that rural people become propelled onto the international scene without first developing loyalties to the nation. Industrial farmers in Kansas sternly warn the housewives of Seattle that they will have to compete with Russians for wheat, conveniently forgetting who pays to maintain parity pricing when economic trouble strikes.

A second major change in our circumstances is that new industries do not demand the same social conditions as did old ones. For the century and a half before World War II, industries could not be established unless a series of narrowly related events also occurred, nurturing the idea that factories were good in themselves. Industry "demanded" education to train its new cadres of managers and workers, cities to house the laborers of all stations, road and rail networks to open the hinterland and tie country to city, and a political structure permitting people and their organizations to be mobilized for new tasks that would also allow them to consume differently. One result was supposed to be that the popular loyalty to community was enlarged—an essential element in nation-building. This kind of technical change promoted specialization, based as it was on highly specific technical knowledge and a sharp division between production and consumption.

The postwar industries, however, assume that managerial and technical skills are equally useful in most enterprises, no matter what their type. They do not "demand" masses of skilled and semi-skilled labor, terrestrial communications nets for the movement of people, or great concentrations of workers grouped conveniently close to rivers and railheads. To produce industrially, then, the great modern cities are no longer technically necessary. People are not faced with the necessity of learning to live together in an urbane fashion in order to manufacture automobiles or toasters. The new industrialization *permits* urbanization and national social skills to develop more effectively than the old industrialization did, but it does not *require* them. We are reminded, then, that industrialization does not make modern industrial man. Instead, we are forced back to the truism that men—modern or otherwise—make industries.

A closely related change is that universal education is no longer required for industrial production, but may well be the key to reasoned consumption. Self-regulating, self-correcting, and capital-intensive manufacturing processes need few persons for their maintenance and feeding, but their managers thirst for great masses to use their products. This new fact of economic life is clearly seen in developing countries, where huge industrial plants can be built in the entire absence of local engineering and accountancy schools, or even trade schools. If such educational facilities are created, it is only because those countries choose to do so for political reasons, not because economic efficiency mandates it.

A fourth critically important disjunction is that economic growth no longer necessarily promotes social mobility, at least in an upward direction. Simple population expansion can permit the social structure to remain unchanged as an economy ramifies. Or, persons can move laterally from one kind of occupation to another without changing their place in the pecking order. At the same time, when social mobility does occur, the attitudes of those who are moving do not necessarily change in expected ways. As class and "class consciousness" do not fall into neatly correlative arrangements, so mobility and ideas about social openness, relativism, and experimentalism also just do not accompany each other. Rather, the tendency seems to be that those who are moving around in society pick up the values of the group they adhere to. The middle classes do not automatically establish the conditions for stability and democracy which old-fashioned theories about development expected them to do. What Dickens knew a long time ago, some social scientists are just beginning to suspect.

American politics has been extraordinarily perturbed in recent years by one crucial failure in an expected relationship—in the idea that schooling has a decisive effect on one's chances for occupational success, and thus that education can be used as a vehicle for overcoming the injustices of racial and other segregations in American society. I shall examine this issue in detail later, but it should be evident even at this early stage of the discussion that sensitive political men should have suspected the difficulty: pushing here won't make things neatly pop out there. And had they known this obvious truth, they also would not have abandoned democratic practice, which in turn would have helped them to think more clearly.

This shedding of the causal ties among various aspects of our social life is a consequence of our growing social skills, as well as of new technology. But these two aspects of our ingenuity do not necessarily proceed hand in hand. The North Vietnamese gave proof to us all that a victorious modern army can be built on what was by any *quantitative* measure a rural, traditional society. It is amazing, but true and heartening, that a society can develop a *qualitative,* industrial, national life in the almost total absence of the physical industries themselves. The essential lesson we should draw from these obvious but little understood facts is that the links in our society are made by us, and not by things. The links are "suggested" by objective situations, abilities, understandings, cultures—but we take the "suggestions" and make them into commandments if we are supine, or conveniences if we are malleable and want to live with as little social illogic as possible.

If societies did not function this way, then there would be no use talking about reason and the freedom to use it. Democracy would be but a form of governance designed to fool people into acquiescence, and it would have nothing to do with seeking the fruits of public discussion and consensual agreement in deciding how we shall give shape to our social lives. If industries did "produce" modern men, if cities did "produce" urbane people, if rural areas did "produce" country bumpkins, if education did "produce" the occupational success of the meritorious, then there would be few problems to debate, and the machine long since would have found its well-oiled equilibrium. Democracy is a process for injecting both reason and power into public decisions. But why worry about reason and power if the situation does it for us, if we are "produced" by things around us and have no hand in making ourselves? Yet it is precisely because so many expect the society to work mechanically that we have so many failures; then the need for a politics of democratic decision becomes all the more obvious, a politics that allows us to choose alternative ways of organizing ourselves and have them accepted as working but temporary solutions. If we are not "produced" by external forces, then we cannot do without the reason and the power to make our own laws of adjustment.

The point is that democracy as a system using empowered reason is *practical*. It answers to the "real" situation by assuming that history is ours to continue and ordering how we ourselves create the future's reality. It also assumes man's sovereignty. It is "hardheaded," because it takes for granted that social organization and reason are basic elements in any construction of social reality. The failure to organize reason and summon power on a societywide basis is counterproductive, inefficient, impractical, and wasteful, and leads to mistakes, to the idea that we live in a world of scarcity, inflexible limits, ever-impending disaster. The popular view, however, is that the world is precisely that—an overcrowded trap in which we cannot afford to be democratic. The truth is that we can afford to be nothing other than democratic. The counsels of despair are advanced by people who do not understand the social bases of the creation of knowledge, nor the social conditions in which one uses knowledge to change limits, the constants within which effective action is undertaken. Social tragedians take the status quo as a given, and see no solution but the use of force to hold together a world impoverishing itself with its insatiable appetite for the production of new people. This unreasoning pessimism provides the rationale for the ultimate destruction of the democratic vision.

The Illogic of the Straitened Mind Technology freaks, Doomsday criers, and faithless democrats are busily at work diagnosing the ills of America—all of them sharing dark visions, a profound mistrust of their fellow citizens, and a shocking lack of understanding of either the philosophical bases of a democratic order or the evolution of social processes. I have named the three types in the order in which they move from simplism and egocentrism to confusing complexity and goodwill. Even

74

though they fold into each other because they are all Utilitarian and thus mechanistic in their premises, let us take them one at a time for the sake of clarity.

Little attention need be paid to anyone who ascribes autonomous power to technology, whether to praise or condemn it. We have already spent sufficient time discrediting the idea that a computer has a soul or a will, or that a tractor decides for itself what it will do to the fellow who mounts it. Why otherwise sane persons can think people must become the unredeemable slaves of their own creations is a question that may be worth a short further exploration, however. It should also be mentioned that Marxists have been no less prone to technological determinism than others. For example, Georg Lukacs complained strongly about his colleagues who would take technology out of its historical social context:

. . . if technique is not conceived as a moment of the existing system of production, if its development is not explained by the development of the social forces of production (and this is what needs clarification), it is just as much a transcendent principle, set over against man, as "nature," climate, environment, raw materials, etc. Nobody doubts that at every determinate stage of the development of the productive forces, which determine the development of technique, technique retroactively influences the productive forces. . . . But it is altogether incorrect and unmarxist to separate technique from the other ideological forms and to propose for it a self-sufficiency from the economic structure of society.[1]

Taking technology out of society and giving it autonomous causal power creates amorality. If the potential ability to do something determines that the something will *necessarily* be done, then where is personal and group responsibility? In practice, we often impersonalize culpability by saying technology "forces" someone to act in a given way, but this scrubbing away of personal guilt does not equally scrub away the enjoyment of personal reward. Military men are especially favored in this way.

Recently a primitivist reaction *against* technology has arisen; it is no more sensible than, or logically any different from, the glorifications of technology.

A primary characteristic of the antitechnologists is the way in which they refer to "technology" as a thing, or at least a force, as if it had an existence of its own. In this they take their cue from [Jacques] Ellul. "Technique has become autonomous," he writes. "It has fashioned an omniverous world which obeys its own laws. . . ." This is not just a figure of speech; it is a serious definition. Repeatedly Ellul emphasizes that "technique pursues its own course more and more independently of man." [2]

The effect of both anti- and pro-technology theories is to promote elitism. The "pro" groups want to elevate the importance of the scientist and the technician, and pretend that policy decisions can be simply technical—as if they were not also a subjective matter involving the creative use of taste and preference to magnify the richness and meaning of life. The "anti" groups are offended in their sensibilities by the hurly-burly of a world just beginning to learn what to do with its new scientific powers, and with the many innovations that are certain to continue to flow. They want to call a halt—but how? They want to get rid of mass society—but how, without getting rid of the masses themselves? They want an end to industrial civilization—but how, without returning to the misery, loneliness, and aching teeth of the medieval age? The antitechnologists have gone so far in seeing the machine as god that they deny their power to do more than luxuriate in a petulant act of disavowal.

. . . where we require clear thinking and courage, the antitechnologists offer us fantasies and despair. Where we need an increase in mutual respect, they exhibit hatred for the powerful and contempt for the weak. The times demand more citizen activism, but they tend to recommend an aloof disengagement. We surely could use a sense of humor, but they are in the grip of an unrelenting dolefulness. [3]

The existential *tristesse* of the technology debaters is as nothing, however, compared with the black gloom of the Doomsday analysts. They are the ones who tell us that if things go on as they are within the present array of circumstances, then we shall soon run out of petroleum, food, living space, unpolluted air, ozone, forests, water, and just about everything else except for radioactive wastes, of which we already have a deplorable surplus. Undoubtedly they are correct, within tolerable margins of statistical error, and given the first condition of a static world.

But formal logic tells us that conclusions based on contrary-to-fact premises are necessarily invalid, false. The fallacy in their argument, of course, is their assumption that "the present array of circumstances" will or can continue. In no conceivable way can that premise hold. If the population of India does indeed double by the end of the century, that change alone will "suggest" so many other adjustments in that unhappy country that today's extrapolations from yesterday's data will have no applicability. If oil prices continue to rise as they have for the past three years, Arabs will be able to buy up all the industries and all the arable land in the United States before the end of the century. The if's march on and on, and each introduces only another fantasy.

Certainly it is correct to be concerned about pollution, uncontrolled population expansion, and the many other manifestations of a world which has little or no control over itself. But if one's worry is contained within an acceptance of things essentially as they are, then one is doomed to envision humanity either in a lemmings' march to collective suicide, or in an authoritarian, totally planned world of everlasting scarcity. In the latter scheme imposition of limits on growth becomes the overriding policy concern, rather than the development of means to reestablish accountability and self-control, to foment change to promote the well-being of people—not of economies or special interests.

New techniques are advanced by the more optimistic of the Doomsday school to suggest at least temporary escapes from the growing pressures humanity is putting on the environment. Improvements in agricultural technology and water usage, new and nonpolluting energy sources, and so on are proceeding apace. This work is often admirable, even though the results are not easily predictable when the new inventions fall into the hands of peasants and other perverse people, whose dispositions of the social effects of technical change differ from the propositions of the planners. However, scientific and technical innovators are not making the greatest difference in the attacks on scarcity but, rather, the political inventors.

Only a few short years ago, India and China were always mentioned in the same breath as countries where population growth seemed an insurmountable problem without mass slaughter at one or another stage of the reproductive cycle. Now, however, nobody doubts that feeding, housing, and clothing the Chinese population at acceptable levels of decency is ensured. What remained unchanged in China's circumstances obviously were its land and its physical resources, and even its rate of population increase. What changed to some extent was the technology the Chinese people could bring to bear on its resources. But what changed most dramatically was its social organization, the ways in which the Chinese grouped themselves for the purposes of growth, not mere survival. The question is not whether social organizations can be devised that will provide for basic wants in education and culture as well as for the satisfaction of animal needs; we have irrefutable proof that societies can do so except in the geographically most benighted of lands—the proof is that some have done the job. As yet out of our grasp is the achievement of the freely self-governing society—and thus more decent as well as more productive and self-controlling people. As it is, recent successes in material development have been accompanied by the installation of dictatorships that invite unreason in the developmental process, and impede the growth of self-sustaining relations between a responsible people and their responsive and accountable governance.

If the Doomsday addicts really care so single-mindedly about survival as their analyses suggest, then the appropriate political solution for them must be in the direction of Maoism, or in the direction of the North Vietnamese and the Cubans, who have essentially solved their health, education, housing, clothing, and feeding problems. But the pessimists are Utilitarians; to them all societies are but input-output mechanisms; so they think Mao is only an Asian George Washington. As the technological determinists breathe the life of Moloch into their machinery, the systems-analysts infuse their mythic creatures with the craven and crass spirit of physical survival. They can only see people scrabbling for the distribution of what materially is, and not the possibilities for different definitions of needs and satisfactions and varied social ways of going about the creation of values and the mechanisms of production, distribution, and consumption.

Remember, too, that faddishness accompanies such social analysis. Only a few short years ago it was affluence, not poverty, that was in the air. In the 1950s and early 1960s, many brows furrowed over how to handle the "surplus" production of our factories and farms and how to occupy people with free time on their hands. Even further back, in the 1930s, popular magazines were telling the world that there was barely enough petroleum left to get through the next world war. Italy and Germany were cited as the grave examples of population overcrowding, and "manifest destiny" was seen in the *Drang nach Osten* of the Germans and the Ethiopian and Libyan adventures of the Italians; that expansionism was supposed to be but the natural, normal, necessary consequence of populations bound to find their *Lebensraum*. Strange, but who now thinks of Germany and Italy as overpopulated? False cries of "wolf" should not prevent our understanding that the wolf may indeed show up, but they should lead us to doubt the trustworthiness of the nervous announcers of our fate.

We must take much more seriously the views of those with little faith in social ability to meet the problems of scarcity with either efficiency or respect for human dignity. These persons do not fall into the vulgar mistakes we have just despatched. Their worry is much better placed: it is simply that, for a variety of reasons, they think we cannot pull ourselves together to evade the maelstrom. Their evidence is that we have so far done so badly in our contemporary political lives, despite our scientific successes, that one can expect little in general, and even less in the saving of the democratic orders that they rightly hold so precious.

Robert L. Heilbroner, who now has such a dark view, writes:

We have become aware that rationality has its limits for engineering social change and that those limits are much narrower than we had thought; that many economic and social problems lie outside the scope of our accustomed instruments of policy-making; that growth does not bring about certain desired ends or arrest certain undesired trends.

Hence in place of the brave talk of the Kennedy generations of managerialists—not to mention the prophets of progress or of a benign dialectical logic of events—there is now a recrudescence of an intellectual conservatism that looks askance at the possibilities for large-scale social engineering, stressing the innumerable cases—for example, the institutionalization of poverty through the welfare system, or the exacerbation of racial friction through the efforts to promote racial equality—in which the consequences of well-intentioned acts have only given rise to other, sometimes more formidable problems than those which they had set out to cure.[4]

This statement, like the Doomsday projections, is correct *if read precisely and narrowly*. Certainly social engineering has not achieved its predicted ends, "our accustomed instruments of policy-making" have not served us, and many well-motivated projects have come to grief. My disagreement is with the implication, pursued in the remainder of Heilbroner's text, that the failures are unavoidable given the nature of our situation. Still, intellectual conservatism has indeed seized upon us, and many persons are turning against reformism, because the serendipitous effects of change have not been predicted or controlled, and we seem to do more harm than good with much that we attempt out of generous inspiration.

But if the ideas which inspired our methods of change envisioned society as pinched, cramped, and animalistic, how can we achieve the generous and devout societies we say we seek? The very ideas prompting the use of such words as "social engineering" falsify social reality, and thus belie the very practicality as well as the ostensible idealism of such social planning. As events betray the managerialists and crises occur, they are forced into coherence. Then their impulses to goodwill are revealed as mere paternalistic charity, not as a true conviction about the nature of being. The managerial engineers are then seen for what they were all along: tinkerers fiddling with problems whose solutions demand originality, system-changing creativity instead of system-maintaining tuning.

Most of today's soured democrats have moved, therefore, from favoring managed reform to proposing managed holding-the-line. We must enter into their arguments in some depth, for they think in ways that run almost entirely counter to democratic politics as a process—even though they ostensibly argue that the only political system worth fighting for, now or in the future of America, is democracy. For example, one such diagnostician wrote the following sentences in the name of plumping for democracy:

> The spread of knowledge about politics may . . . reduce the amount of well-meant but often harmful interference by citizens in the workings of political institutions. A public which understands the nature and necessity of politics may perhaps be more willing than one that does not to allow politicians to do their work without obstruction. Such a public may be more appreciative of the social values of this work. . . . And it may be more aware of the risks it runs of damaging, or perhaps even of destroying, a tolerable system by attempting reforms the full effects of which cannot be foreseen.[5]

This was written in the early 1960s, before we appreciated how fully "developmentalists" abroad and reformers at home had been defeated, and before the racial and student troubles of that decade reached their peaks. Imagine, then, the disquiet caused the managerialists by those happenings, and by the government's attendant attempts to ameliorate social restlessness. Consequently it is natural that these scholars should now begin to ask whether democracies are "governable" at all. But the query itself is undemocratic: the classical democratic question is how to return "*self*-governability" to differentiated institutions and to citizens.

The discouraged democrats construct the case in the opposite way and in a way opposed to the thrust of the American revolutionary ethos. Samuel P. Huntington has written one of the most interesting statements of this contrasting view. He begins his exposition by asserting that the troubles of the 1960s were an evidence of a "democratic distemper"—of too much democracy![6]

The 1960s witnessed a dramatic renewal of the democratic spirit in America. The predominant trends of that decade involved the challenging of the authority of established political, social, and economic institutions, increased popular participation in and control over those institutions, a reaction against the concentration of power in the executive branch of the federal government and in favor of the reassertion of the power of Congress and of state and local government, renewed commitment to the idea of equality on the part of intellectuals and other elites, the emergence of "public interest" lobbying groups, increased concern for the rights of and provision of opportunities for minorities and women to participate in the polity and economy, and a pervasive criticism of those who possessed or were even thought to possess executive power or wealth.[7]

Huntington then proceeds to argue that Americans are demanding and receiving more benefits from government than ever before—this paradoxically accompanied by a "substantial decrease in governmental authority." He continues, "The vitality of democracy in the 1960s raised questions about the governability of democracy in the 1970s," and finally puts the matter boldly, "Does an increase in the vitality of democracy *necessarily* have to mean a decrease in the governability of democracy?" [8] Huntington answers in the affirmative. For among other reasons American democracy does not have enough *lèse majesté* inherent in it. "Democracy is more of a threat to itself in the United States than it is in either Europe or Japan where there still exist residual inheritances of traditional and aristocratic values. The absence of such values in the United States produces a lack of balance in society. . . ."

He concludes as follows:

The vulnerability of democratic government in the United States . . . comes . . . from the internal dynamics of democracy itself in a highly educated, mobilized, and participant society. "Democracy never lasts long," John Adams observed. "It soon wastes, exhausts, and murders itself. There never was a democracy yet that did not commit suicide." That suicide is more likely to be the product of overindulgence than of any other cause. A value which is normally good in itself is not necessarily optimized when it is maximized. We have come to recognize that there are potentially desirable limits to economic growth. There are also potentially desirable limits to the indefinite extension of political democracy. Democracy will have a longer life if it has a more balanced existence." [9]

I place primary responsiblility for our troubles on those with the greatest amounts of overt, day-to-day power in society. Huntington puts it on the victims of their power, ethnics, intellectuals, certain women, the poor—on those who have the least day-to-day institutionalized effectiveness. Huntington thinks the government is giving more than ever; I think society and the government are in many ways giving us less—less frankness, honesty, meaningful involvement, and for many, less work, less dignity, less hope. I think of limits as I do the banks of a canal; Huntington thinks of them as the four walls, ceiling, and floor of a cell. Huntington explicitly rejects Al Smith's maxim that when democracy is in trouble we need more of it; I explicitly accept that proposition. I think the lack of a tradition of deference to aristocratic rank is a good thing, there may be too much deference of this kind even in America, especially when it comes to the presidency; Huntington thinks there is too little of it. I think government should be loyal to its citizens; Huntington never mentions this aspect of political responsiveness and responsibility. Huntington cites Adams and Madison; I rest my case with Montesquieu, Rousseau, and Jefferson. Thus, it should not be surprising that where Huntington sees in the "democratic distemper" of the 1960s, "too much" democracy, I see a failure of democracy, not enough of it.

Burning cities, race riots, marches on Washington, the occupation of university buildings, and restless movements of social protest certainly may be evidences that the people have inchoate democratic aspirations. And it is true that much of the public temper of these years profoundly reflects America's democratic *culture*. But it is not a manifestation of a democratic *order*. There would be no need for people to take their politics to the streets if they could be effective through their parties, votes, representatives, and interest groups. Using his systems-analysis metaphor, Huntington argues that the "input" functions of government—political parties and the like—have been losing authority, while the output functions—benefits and so forth—have been increasing. To continue with the figure of speech, I suggest that the "black box" in the middle, the government, is pinching off the "inputs" with inflexibility, dishonesty, and unresponsiveness, while it doles out the "outputs" by way of sops, favors, payoffs, and other surrenders of a straightforward, respectable politics of austere republicanism.

Riots and demonstrations, sabotage and assassination, official violence, and *guerrillosmo* are dreadfully common events these days. Why should they be labelled the evidence of a "democratic distemper" and not the symptoms of political maladies, the shrieks of people trying to be heard? When only the insane cry out, then one may suspect the state is not overly at variance with the citizenry. But when the cries come from everyone, as they have in the United States, one can easily imagine that the primary trouble lies with our institutions and their leaders, not with the weakest among us.

By and large, elitist democrats remain totally silent on issues of power; they maintain that equality refers only to "natural" political rights and nothing else; [10] they show little sympathy or understanding of the plight of less advantaged groups; and they bear particular animosity toward "intellectuals," as though they, themselves, were not among the most honored members of that confraternity. They also dislike students with rambunctious political ideas, and delight in pointing out that the classroom and the laboratory are poor places indeed to practice democracy. The unsigned introduction to the Trilateral Commission Report, of which the Huntington diagnosis is a part, puts the case against the intellectuals in pure form:

The development of an "adversary culture" among intellectuals has affected students, scholars, and the media. Intellectuals are, as Schumpeter put it, "people who wield the power of the spoken and the written word, and one of the touches that distinguish them from other people who do the same is the absence of direct responsibility for public affairs." In some measure, the advanced industrial societies have spawned a stratum of value-oriented intellectuals who often devote themselves to the derogation of leadership, the challenging of authority, and the unmasking and delegitimation of established institutions, their behavior contrasting with that of the also increasing numbers of technocratic and policy-oriented intellectuals. In an age of widespread secondary school and university education, the pervasiveness of the mass media, and the displacement of manual labor by clerical and professional employees, this development constitutes a challenge to democratic government which is, potentially at least, as serious as those posed in the past by the aristocratic cliques, fascist movements, and communist parties. [11]

By this time the outrageousness of that statement should not surprise us. Put aside the fact that the Founding Fathers were all "value-oriented intellectuals" who challenged authority openly and violently. Let us not ask how many of the "mass media" devoted themselves to exposing the syndrome we call "Watergate," or how many of them are really concerned with the "delegitimation" of what their owners and managers and editors hold dear. Don't press for a definition of "adversary culture," or ask how all these terrible students, scholars, and news reporters are menacing Americanism as much as "aristocratic cliques, fascist movements, and communist parties." In other words, let's forget for the moment our history, common courtesy, caution in distinguishing among different persuasions of intellectuals, and small matters of overstatement. What leaves me perplexed is where the authors leave room for disagreement. We are supposed not to ask for too much, talk too much, dissent too much, be value-oriented, or think about the legitimacy of established institutions. Well, what *are* we supposed to do?

It seems that the curdled democrat believes that what we should do is be quiet and vote for our warden every four years. And if we don't like what we have "chosen," than we should remain silent and wait for the next election to roll around to vote for another keeper; if we don't we shall be treated harshly by Daddy Warbucks, who might not then be willing to hand over his paddle to his elected successor. Perhaps, though, we are already menaced by that situation, and perhaps part of the "democratic distemper" is caused by awareness of the threat. Certainly the punitive chastisements addressed toward New York City by the national government would seem to support that possibility.

One commentator on the present scene puts on our diapers as follows?

. . . two conservative Republican presidents have brought the United States to the point where national planning is an emergent institutional reality . . . Regardless of its local consequences, new federalism has turned American democracy into a national technocracy free to plan and manage its domestic and foreign objectives from a global perspective without effective popular participation. Or—to draw on President Nixon's characterization of the American people as children in need of a strong father—under the new federalism, Washington's technocratic patriarch retains the power over critical national choices and leaves America's children to play, more or less democratically, with an allowance of local toys. If the patriarch decides that any city has overspent its allowance, its spanking will be severe, its democratic privileges will be suspended and its allowance will be "seasonally administered" and terminable at will. As Secretary Simon told the Senate Banking Committee, he should be put in charge of any New York aid "to determine that the city was irrevocably and unalterably on the path to fiscal responsibility. Such aid should be so punitive in its terms and so painful that no other city not facing absolute disaster would think of applying for help." [12]

Of course. The authors of the Trilateral Commission Report and their intellectual colleagues are no longer democrats. They propose national technical planning, they want to maintain elitist governance legitimated by periodic "popular" ratification, and they have a romantic attachment to civil liberties although they are no longer conceptually certain why that should be so. In other words, for the present they are humane technocrats. They say that they are pessimistic about the future of "democracy." The only conclusion I reach is that they are pessimistic about the chances of keeping their technocracy humane. So am I, so am I.

Now only one last task remains to these disguised technocrats in their usurpation of the concept, "democracy"; with one master stroke they seek to wipe out their intellectual opposition, nominate themselves and their compeers as the legitimate heirs of established power, and destroy the historical sense and tradition of our revolutionary and constitutionalist founders. They accomplish this coup by basing their legitimacy on the ostensible centrality of knowledge, which would of course give them unique importance in our present situation. Here they enter upon treacherous ground, however, for many people have knowledge. So they must and do suggest that only one kind of knowledge is politically and socially useful today, and that all too many of us have access to the university-factories that "produce" knowledge of the wrong kinds. Their argument can be easily traced.

The first premise of the pseudo-democratic, technocratic argument is that in "post-industrial" society abstract and theoretical knowledge is "the matrix of invention." [13] This premise is in turn based on a historical assessment that technocratic, neo-democratic society already exists, that the future is already with us, so to speak. Therefore, no useful or desirable purpose can be served by debating the bounds of what already is. Indeed, because "post-industrialism" *is* the revolution of our times, arguing about or against it is reactionary, counter-revolutionary, in opposition to the historical moment.[14] The only useful kind of knowledge concerns what one has to know to administer the new system into its full bloom. Such knowledge is essentially of a technical, problem-solving sort—not Utopian, dangerous if concerned with alternative ideal-states or other visions, and necessarily scarce. That is, only few minds are capable of the refinement required for technical policymaking. These scarce intellects will necessarily be trained in universities. But as these favored ones will be few, there need not be many truly important universities. S. M. Lipset is entirely frank about it. He says that the "primary function of the university is scholarship, which includes rigorous education, not politics or therapy. . . . There can only be a faculty and students, although there will be thousands of accredited institutions of higher education." [15] Those other baby-sitting institutes will create difficulties, for they will produce "value-oriented intellectuals" instead of "technocratic and policy-oriented intellectuals"—not my words, remember. The resulting problem is that while only the few can govern, the many who have attended school have pretensions to governance. Unfortunately, these emerging "classes" of value-oriented intellectuals are opposed to the proper and fitting leaders, inhibiting the more functionally useful minds from carrying out their work.[16] If the "functionally useless" are allowed to live, it is only because the elites need people against whom to measure themselves, and to provide a recruitment pool for their successors, to be chosen in meritocratic competition.

These postulations gut democracy. They destroy its structure. The technical and policy-intellectuals do not allow room for checks and balances, since they claim to be the only ones sufficiently able to know how to administer our increasingly complex machinery. They destroy Liberalism's grand political idea: in the works of Locke and Adam Smith, institutional behavior is properly thought to be ethically motivated, while the technocrats elevate the amoral god of Utility to the altar. They destroy the central idea of democratic governance: the democratic project is self-governance within discrete but interacting spheres, a self-governing people ceding ultimate authority over inter-institutional disputes to the state; but the technocrats want to impose national and even global planning. They destroy the idea of political community: Democratic theory is bound up with the idea of national communities of mutually respecting citizens, while the success of the technocratic vision would make idiosyncracy powerless. They destroy democracy's ethic: Classical democratic theory calls for a surrender of individual political will to the political community in return for equality before the laws, while the technocrats ask for surrender to a state that will maximize the power of the holders of technical knowledge. They destroy democracy's dynamic quality: Democracy contains the dream that men can move society toward an adjustment with the "naturally" good, while the technocrats emphasize *being* and positively reject *becoming* in any sense other than optimizing the extant situation. And, lastly, the technocrats destroy America's patriotic vision: we have thought highly of our founding generations of thinkers and activists, while the technocrats reduce them to "value-oriented intellectuals" or falsify them into "intellectual policy-makers." There is no licit way to shrink America's first leaders into bookkeepers. The Founding Fathers created a nation, no matter how far away from their varied hopes it may have drifted; they did not merely think up and implement "policy."

If the ideas of the technocrats triumph, we shall survive neither as a national people nor as a democracy. Their search for Utility drives them inevitably to globalize all their concepts, to suggest that nations will become as sick as the inner city already is within the United States. This sort of "rationalization" can lead only to an equally low standard for the "functionally useless" throughout the world, and an equally high standard for all those who create and manage our scarcity. Democracy vanishes, of course, the moment its survival depends only upon the goodwill of the governors and their technical henchmen. It is of critical importance to our national survival and our democratic temper, then, that we do not permit ourselves to be frightened by minds that have lost vision. They describe neither present reality nor future possibility. Nor should they be allowed to escape responsiblility for their own incompetence by our accepting their argument that all would be well were it not for the messy "overundereducated" citizenry cluttering up the polity.

What has recently been said of Presidents Johnson and Nixon is also true of the academic technocrats. ". . . John Adams [said] a long time ago: 'Power always thinks it has a great soul and vast views beyond the comprehension of the weak and that it is doing God's service when it is violating all His laws.' The atomic bomb isn't to blame for the madness of machismo; it's power itself that drives so many Presidents balmy, and it's a miracle that more of them haven't led us into the straits of the Johnson-Nixon years." [17]

Our recent presidents have tended to think that power is a physical bundle of armaments, and the technocratic professors have come to think that knowledge is a package of skills that can be "produced" and doled out to all competent comers. As techniques are given their own life, so is knowledge—and both become divorced from reason. I have already quoted Cassirer pointing out that in the eighteenth-century reason was understood ". . . not as a sound body of knowledge, principles, and truths, but as a kind of energy, a force which is fully comprehensible only in its agency and effects. What reason is, and what it can do, can never be known by its results but only by its function." Democracy needs functioning reason, or it cannot have movement and an effective citizenry. Knowledge without reason is insanity. For a reasoning society, we need Big Tens and West Chester State Teachers' College as much as we do Berkeley, Chicago, and Harvard. Can you imagine being governed by Berkeley's Sociology department or Harvard's Department of Government?

The technocrats' desire to make their educational attainments the fount of power is a common thread in American life. More than any other of our social institutions, education has borne the brunt of our contradictory hopes and inhibitions. If as a nation we are undecided on how to think about reason, knowledge, class, nation, race, occupations, or ideology, at least there seems general agreement that education is a good thing and vital to democracy. But it is also the institution which brings the family into direct relation with the state. That is, in formal education the most intimate of our institutions meets the most general, and is expected to answer to our desires both for personal immortality through our children and for cultural immortality through our nation. The educational establishment, then, is the most sensitive test of the quality of our hopes and our politics.

From Coleman to Rousseau What Americans think schools should do and what they actually do are two quite different matters for Utilitarian minds, two quite similar matters for Liberal-Enlightenment thinkers. We shall have to pick the problem apart carefully, though, for as with all else in American politics, the mix of ambiguities is bedazzling.

The Enlightenment view was that the purpose of education is to form generally cultured persons, able to create and work in a "field of reason." Such people make their own ways, create their own histories, build their factories and cities and states. They are the wellspring of all else, since in the wisdom of that time, value can flow from no place other than the minds and muscles of people. Jefferson encapsulated the view in his aphorism, "If a nation expects to be ignorant and free, in a state of civilization, it expects what never was and never will be."

The Utilitarian view is that education is a link in the chain creating the factors of production. For the Utilitarian education is not formative of the person, but rather trains, imparts skills to generate the "labor" and "management" components of the land-labor-capital-management quartet which produces our worldly rewards. Educational planning, then, cannot be divorced from the occupational slots which the trained are being prepared to fill. As the formula goes, manpower studies—projections of the need for "skills," not persons—are preconditions for adequate educational planning. We need to know how many mechanics, doctors, veterinarians, and housewives society "needs" before we can know how to "allocate educational resources." If we assume that labor is a commodity, then what is more logical than to see schools as factories producing the commodity?

In our aspirations for our educational practice, America mixes the Liberal eighteenth and the Utilitarian nineteenth centuries. These two conflicting educational purposes are further confounded by racial and class issues. Schools are asked not only to form persons and produce skills, but also to provide for equalization of condition and equality of opportunity. In the 1890s the Supreme Court, in the famous *Plessy* v. *Ferguson* decision, exempted schools from having to reflect Liberal guarantees of equality of condition. Instead, the Court approved "separate but equal" facilities, sanctioning the racial segregation which legitimated the self-cozening idea that equality of opportunity was enough, no matter how different the starting points of the individual competitors in society's increasingly unequal game of making it. Sixty years later, in the mid-1950s, the Court reversed itself, holding that to be separated was to be substantively unequal, even if society had been honest enough to provide objectively equal facilities for both black and white. Of a sudden, America's educational system was asked to add equality of condition to its other goals of providing equality of opportunity, general education for citizenship, and job-training. We have ever been prone to expect more from our schools than from any other social institution:

The American public schools are, in the opinion of the people of the United States, basic and necessary parts of our democracy. We are convinced that they must, and we hope that they do, provide equal opportunity for every child. This means that those at the bottom can compete through education for life's prizes with those at the top. All that is needed are brains, a will to do, hard work, and plenty of ambition. In our faith every aspiring student may not have a marshal's baton in his knapsack, but in his public schooling he does have an equal chance with everyone else for the White House.[18]

When the decision was judicially reached that the American legal system could no longer countenance the systematic exclusion of ten percent of the national population, what easier and more natural step could be taken than to assign to education the task of undoing the wrongs done against blacks since 1619? The problems triggered by the *Brown* v. *Board of Education* decision were predictably profound. Most parents hope for redemption through their children, and schools first take their progeny long before they are ready to leave the nest for self-sustaining flight. Parents of all colors see schooling as intimately involved with eventual success—through upward mobility for the less favored, and by maintenance of status and privilege for the better off. But more is expected from schools than awarding badges and certifying status. The educational system is a major repository of society's values, and the primary means by which society creates and passes on its cultural heritage, including not only techniques and philosophical wisdom, but also ordered notions of right and wrong.

The Supreme Court slowly and cautiously entered into this sensitive bundle of social synapses in its classical reading of the Constitution, but there is little reason to think it did not also implicitly expect a democratically positive chain of events to flow from the decision. Improvement of the educational situation of racially and otherwise depressed groups would heighten their chances for occupational success. Better jobs, better pay, more participation, more power, greater civic responsibility, better chances for the next generation, and so on would add up to the greater good of the greatest number through the success of the fittest.

Ten years later a massive report appeared saying that all this would never happen: The kind and quality of schooling has little or no effect on occupational success. The Coleman Report was called a "formidable achievement" in an anthology of commentary on the work, which summed up the major finding in these blunt words: "The pathbreaking quality of the . . . [Report] had to do with its analysis of variations in school facilities to variations in levels of academic achievement. It reported so little relation as to make it almost possible to say there was none." [19] The study also found that if the kind and quality of education did not affect the cognitive skills of children, they also did not affect their chances for jobs upon graduation. Coleman concluded that the major influence in both dimensions—learning and occupational success—was family. The only minor effect the type of school seemed to have on learning and jobs was a weak association derived from schoolmates. That is, scholastically smarter and better-placed youngsters seemed to help pull up their less blessed fellows. Differences among schools themselves—their teachers, erasers, books, location, architecture, color of their blackboards—seems to matter not at all. Ergo, education in itself could not be used to break the circle of color, poverty, unemployment, poverty, color.

Naturally, this study caused great dismay. So, it was tested— the best known of those repeat studies being by Christopher Jencks and some of his associates in 1970. Jencks and his colleagues, to their great disappointment, came out with the same findings, concluding, "We have not . . . been very successful in explaining most of these inequalities [among educational opportunities, cognitive skills, educational credentials, occupational status, income, and job satisfaction]. The association between one variety of inequality and another is usually quite weak, which means that equalizing one thing is unlikely to have much effect on the degree of inequality in other areas." [20] These studies do not say that nothing is learned in school, that education is not needed for successful work, or that for some students schools do not make mobility possible. All that they say—and accurately—is that on a mass, probabilistic basis, action to equalize and integrate schools will only marginally affect the cognitive skills of disadvantaged children; thus, schools do not trigger the process that can carry underprivileged students upward through a permanently changed and more equalitarian social structure. And the studies also point out that rich and poor number in their ranks both the bright and the dumb, and thus social status does not correlate with individual potential. Lastly, they imply what we all know: The surest way to become a millionaire is to be born to one.

What is surprising is that these studies were surprising. Aside from giving us the obvious information that class and status matter in the United States despite our national ideology, the studies reaffirm a basic truth: In complex societies major facets of social life do not fit together in straight lines; to change one aspect is not to change others in given ways. This very openness of structure should be a cause for joy. And it is probably a major result of the vast amount of schooling that has been for so long available in the United States. If Coleman, Jencks, and others had asked not what schooling did for the occupational structure, but what it did for the students, they would have been politically as well as scientifically more positive. To put it in other words, if they had seen schools not as places that develop skills, but as institutions that help persons to create themselves, they would have found strikingly different results, including an explanation of why "equalizing one thing is unlikely to have much effect on the degree of inequality in other areas."

As it is, these studies "explain" inequality by saying that it is the result of inequality. The implication is that the inequality of the underprivileged is to blame for the inability of the poor and colored to compete. The inequality of the better placed is not mentioned. To define the problem as one of underprivilege, and not of privilege, is to repeat, albeit in less pejorative tones, the smug self-excuse of the technocrats—that the weak make their own situation. Obviously, the nexus between the inequalities of both privilege and deprivation begins to give meaningful shape to the problem, and to the distribution of relative responsibility.

Rousseau's general idea of the matter, like that of some contemporary psychologists, is that there are times in a person's life when certain subject matters can be learned and other times when they simply cannot. He thought that as people move from childhood and the world of "things" into adolescence, they enter the world of reason, and thus of morality. (For him, there could be no morality—hence responsibility—without the ability to reason.) These ideas have been made much more elaborate and sophisticated with the passage of time, and they have been rediscovered in whole or in part by many different scholars. But a clear pattern seems to be emerging from the varied academic research using diverse conceptual approaches:

· If students can remain in school into adolescence, they seem suddenly to become empathic, able to identify with others across social and cultural distance, and to see public affairs in a relativistic way.

· People who develop these abilities tend to become less predictable in the ordering of their political attitudes. They become more "liberal" in the vulgar sense of that term, or tend toward the political independence of the informed, as distinct from the "independence" of the ignorant.

· Persons with sufficient schooling seem able to tolerate ambiguities. They do not expect or desire society to be formed into tightly knit organic wholes leaving little room for movement. The complexities and lack of neat predictability in their own attitudes are accompanied by a correlative ability to see the

94

ambiguities in others, and in the society as a whole.

· Persons able to see and tolerate ambiguities also create a contradiction in their social lives if their institutional order does not tolerate play, difference, and disjunction. That is, education creates a social ability which a person may not easily tolerate in other areas of his life. Thus, "town-gown" controversies are inevitable. The town and its elders want conformity and staid acceptance of the status quo, and want students to be small versions of the grown-ups they are ostensibly training to become. But the secondary school and the university are scenes of the discovery of freedom. The student makes his first structured break with the parental family (and probably also with formal religion), and he is not yet encumbered with job, political duties, or his own family. He is institutionally freer than he will ever be again, at the very same time that education is teaching him intellectualism—how to remove himself from the narrowness of the accidents of his birth and childhood, and to frame perspectives that permit him to see across social life and time, and even to view himself in these perspectives.

· Persons without schooling well into adolescence seem generally unable to develop these skills.

As in the case of the Coleman and Jencks findings, the kind of school attended does not seem greatly to affect the growth of these abilities. The institutional experience in itself appears to be the catalyst to this self-development of mind and personality, because it provides both institutional freedom and intellectual play. But neither Coleman nor Jencks asks what the total educational experience means to the students; their mind-set sees education as instrumental, a way to achieve other ends, but not as an "expressive" function, something done for its own sake, for the enrichment of people.

These conclusions are supported by studies of many kinds carried out overseas as well as in the United States.[21] Study after study reveals that the more education a person has, the more likely he is to be "liberal" (read "open"), to be abashed at feelings of racism, to think in national and international dimensions, to see public affairs with refinement, to be "conservative" in some specific political views and "liberal" in others, and yet to be able to develop syntheses to bind together his complex set of views—to be "ideological," in other words.

To put the findings another way, it can be said that the political attitudes of the uneducated or the undereducated are very similar to those of grammar-school children in certain respects. Both groups seek for certainty. They cling to familistic and religious values, and want to bend economic, educational, and political behavior to the service of their families and religious beliefs. It is not unfair, then, to say that family-centered and small-group conservatism is the politics of children. That some of these "children" live in the muscular bodies of grown-ups is one of the greatest dangers of our times.

Obviously, not everyone with a university degree develops a relativistic, rationalistic, and changeful set of ideas about life. And not everyone without formal schooling forever clings to the warm verities of a totally ordered and structured universe. The schooled minority with a mania for order provides some of the trickier political ideologies of our days. From their ranks come the technocrats, managerialists, and pseudo-democrats of our country, as well as the systems-analysts of the Soviet Union and the corporatists of recent European political history.

Neither the right nor the left, the educated nor the uneducated, is free of those who try to impose a self-consistent order across the entire spectrum of social life—from family attachments and religious beliefs to economic and political behavior.

Two kinds of minds are abroad in the land. The type that insists on imposing absolute order on everything is entirely predictable. His attitudes fall into a scalar relation: that is, if one element of his thought is known, other elements can be predicted with almost unfailing accuracy. For example, persons who hate blacks have a very high propensity also to hate Jews (if they are not Jews themselves) or Catholics (if they are not Catholics themselves) or Protestants (if they are not Protestants themselves). Minds which harbor racial hatreds also tend to oppose abortion, despise homosexuals, be suspicious of the federal government, and generally support familistic and local values over national, impersonal ones. They also like to paste flags on their car windows. This observation is old in the social sciences, going back to a famous study of the 1940s of what was then called "the authoritarian personality" measured by the "f-scale"—or "fascism-scale." [22] A major criticism directed against that study and subsequent similar findings is that an analogous "d-scale" or "democracy-scale" cannot be found. But that is the very point: people equipped to live democratically do not expect or demand that each piece of their lives will line up with all the other pieces. The statistical reflection is that their attitudes do not fall into scales; knowing "item A" about such minds, one cannot predict "item B" about them. What we *can* predict about the democratic mind is that it sees the whole as different from the sum of the parts; political life has appeals, purposes, and ends different from those of friendship, religion, or family. The scaling mind may have been schooled, but the school experience has not brought it out of the world of things into the world of reason and ethics. The nonscaling mind has become cultured by its education, tempered to resolving ambiguity not by denying or destroying it but by synthesizing it into overall patterns.

We can now recognize the quality of the pseudo-democratic technocratic mind. It has no empathy for the disadvantaged because it cannot see over social distance. It cannot blame leaders and other managers for causing basic problems, for all those men are simply driving a machine. If the road is bumpy, it is because of all those misguided people who are throwing themselves down in front of the wheels. The split between the pseudo-democratic technocrat and the true democrat is not a matter of degree. The schism is qualitative, dividing one way of thought from another way of thought. This crisis of world views suggests that the Utilitarian-Liberal and class-nation clash is now fully ripe. The failure to resolve the conflict will shake apart our educational system—the way we introduce young people to the past and the present, the way we make it possible for persons to learn to become citizens of a democratic state, the only institutional procedure we have for growing the seeds of continuing freedom.

The clash is not between capitalists and socialists, or between the left and the right as these terms are conventionally used. More accurately, it is the opposition between authoritarianism and democracy, slavery and freedom, or, if you prefer, between genuine right and genuine left. All of the industrialized world, whether "capitalist" America or "socialist" Russia, is witness to this struggle between these two different kinds of minds—the truly educated, and the merely trained.

THE
REASON
FOR

FREEDOM

e do not now know, nor have we ever known, whether we are right or wrong. Life's great Uncertainty Principle is that no one can ever be sure whether he is ultimately correct or incorrect in his views of the nature and purpose of life and the universe. This rock-hard unsureness is the best reason for establishing a contained and relativistic system of governance that has as its first principle the separation of what is changeful and secular from what is permanent and sacred. It is man's fate that he live inside his own skull, deciding there how he will create his understandings of the real. Within that inside-of-himself he may decide that he is God's tool, or that only he exists and the rest of mankind are shadows he conjures up for his amusement, or that he is working his head to create a complex amalgam of himself and all the rest of us, carrying along all our cultures and histories. Whatever he may decide, *he* decides. If that is indeed how we are—doomed to dream up evanescent premises that we must pretend are absolute—then we had better make sure to create social arrangements that take account of the inescapable necessity of our being certain only of our primal uncertainty. If we deliver ourselves over to a society dedicated to affirming the truth of a master certainty instead of a master doubt, we must bid farewell to respect for the uniqueness of our personalities—and to democracy.

That I accept an underlying uncertainty should not be taken to mean that I think I am wrong. But I have taken into account the possibility that I may be ultimately totally mistaken about God and man and nature. Of course, you may be as misguided as I. Therefore I must seek to protect myself against your acts of faith, and you against mine. That protection from ourselves is a social matter, not an individual one, for otherwise we should lose society and become hostile beasts in a nasty and brutish world. The social arrangements of decent civil society encourage us to assume the personal responsibility of understanding and explaining ourselves to others, and of making the effort to understand the explanations offered by our fellows.

The only sense in which we can and should reach for certainty is within our systems of explanation. Here, for example, I have sought to escape error in two quite standard ways: by avoiding internal illogicalities in the argumentation, and by positing a way of understanding that is efficient in the sense that more is explained with fewer presuppositions. After all, the less I require others to accept a tangle of faith-premises in order to understand me, the more I remove my thought from "magic" and move it into a realm whose sense can be shared in the here and now. The consequence is that I increase the ability to correct others and to be corrected—to be as "right" as I can within my historical and cultural moment. The more classical way to put it is that I seek to extend the range of reason and, with it, the possibility of sharing minds with my fellows in my time as well as through our histories. To extend our humanness in this way, we need intelligence and openness, assured by a politics that defends the ineluctability of uncertainty—a politics absolutely designed to deny absolutes.

The argument is neither abstruse nor unfamiliar. The American vision and practice propound it in many ways. We know perfectly well that men make laws and thus are "above" them; but we also strive for a government of laws and not of men.

Similarly, we all believe that laws can and should change; yet the legal order requires that laws should be obeyed absolutely while they are in force. Most of us quote with approval the idea that we may loathe what someone else says but we should defend "to the death" his right to speak. Through those conceptual dualisms we make the absolute relative through time, and make the relative absolute in any given moment. When we take a pinpoint moment as absolute, we have leverage for action; when we take the entire structure of our being as relative, we have the chance to change our wills with our minds. The two together provide flexibility and commitment. A democracy can be rested on no other premise and cannot be exercised without that set of abilities.

Only an intellectualizing society of trained minds can abide the idea of ultimate doubt and yet understand and act on the need for temporary absoluteness. Democracy, then, is a political order inconsonant with uncultivated and childish minds because they demand certainty and organic patterns imposed by external laws. The natural condition of the cultivated mind, however, is within a liberating political order—liberating in the sense that people are freed to share across cultural and historical bounds and to continue the creation of their worldly destinies. Science, technology, invention, and the other requisites of material comfort are as dependent upon such liberating creativity as is the nurture of our human spirit. Partial democracy and material wealth have accompanied each other through history to our modern estate; they are still linked, still partners not in convenience but in necessity.

Living democratically demands subtle and discriminating intellectual effort. Living under a tyranny does not, unless one seeks to escape it, of course. The same can be said of democratic and authoritarian theory-building. All authoritarian thinkers build their structures on an easily described, assumed concreteness. They may start with a description of man's nature as a "thing," or with God's word as recorded in one or another "sacred" text, or with some social characteristic they see arising from man's innate "animal nature." Once this given is concretely laid, the elaboration of a self-consistent structure is limited only by the imagination of the architect. Our literature is full of these theories. We have the cyclical determinisms of such as Spengler and Toynbee, and the "great man" theories of Carlyle, and the practices of Hitler. We also have yesterday's proponents of inherited aristocracies, and today's advocates of the "natural" aristocracies of the gifted—our meritocrats and technocrats. These constructions are simple because they are undynamic: They refer to states of being, not of becoming; they talk of the imposition of force, not of the creation of power; they design the superimposition of government, not the melding of governance with self-governance. They are also ultimately pessimistic theories, for they posit immobilism and scarcity not only in our productive devices, but also in the realm of human capacity.

It is useless to ask old-fashioned democratic questions of theorists of authoritarianism, whether they propose "soft" tyranny or "hard." The democratic problematic concerns social change, causality, and dynamism. How is the dictator to save himself and his society from fatal error in a world of ultimate weaponry? What self-corrective devices can be built into tyranny? How can the social power of a dictatorship compare with the massed willingness to live and do together of a freely interacting community of citizens? How can the education needed for members of a complex, interdependent modern economy be squared with the mental torpidity demanded of subjects held in political thralldom? How can the rationalization, the ordering of relations, in a perhaps well-functioning dictatorship be accommodated with the *reason* that must guide the choice of the ends toward which the integrated machine will be put? These questions should not be asked separately. They should be combined, in order to force authoritarians to demonstrate that the "utility," "efficiency," and "order" they all promise can really evolve in a society that does not attempt to maximize the individual and social powers of its competent citizens, a society that does not understand that self-correction must start with our very premises and not be restricted merely to our everyday mistakes.

But this book is not about dictatorship. It is about democracy, a much more difficult subject. It is difficult to think about, difficult to create and maintain, and always threatened by its success. Social freedom invariably creates gains. And these advances in turn invariably create new interests and new powers with which to defend those interests. The unending tyrannies of Nicaragua and Saudi Arabia, say, have created little and need little in the way of social innovation even for their own maintenance. The incredible blazes of social energy given us by the Greek and Italian city-states and the early nation-states, caused by the opening of their citizens' minds, also established interests and means for their defense which eventually came to include carpet bombing, totalitarian dictatorship, and nuclear weapons. The world's most creative societies are also the world's most destructive ones.

Now we have little time or room left for a continuing failure to understand that the first sacrifice to be made for democracy is the unreason of sacred tradition. We must continue to forswear indulgence in unreason, or the rewards of the difficult exercise of reason in freedom will be lost as we seek to preserve our gains instead of the means by which we produced them. This is why we urgently need a reconstruction of a democratic theory of continuing to become ourselves. Both our survival and the justification for our survival depend upon it. So, too, does our material prosperity, which was and ever will be the fruit of our intellectual prosperity, without which decent and productive society cannot exist. This intellectuality, the ability to think ourselves into and out of effective action, is the first victim of authoritarianism, and the ultimate strength of democracy.

. . . Intellectuality includes the human potential to reject and review given parameters, to say "no" to established epistemologies, to introduce qualitatively new ideas and to reflect on intellectual work critically within a given social context. . . . Intellectuality . . . is not a natural endowment nor an asset a person possesses; rather, it is the realization of a potential, usually attained through strenuous effort; it is an achievement that may quickly vanish if the effort is relaxed. . . .[1]

This capacity to stand aside from oneself and others involves a freeing from and a freeing for. That is, intellectualism implies the ability to see outside the confines of one's family, friends, social station, culture, and even historical time. It frees one from the accident of birth. And it frees one to deepen attachments, commitments, and loyalties by reinforcing sentiment with informed reason. But in both the negative and positive senses of freedom, intellectualism has meaning only with reference to society's structures: The "freedom from" is a removal from given social settings; the "freedom to" is an involvement with them. And, in both cases, the ability to exercise freedom is a product not only of personal capacities, training, and knowledge, but also of access to social institutions. No alchemy transmutes knowledge, intellectuality, skills, learning, wisdom, and empathy into power. Conversely, power does not spawn reason. But power and intellectualized, relativizing reason need each other if each is to reach its peak. The mix of the two can be complete only in free societies—in societies where the power deriving from the consensual participation of a total citizenry is the product of the reasoned understanding that the maximum personal difference is promoted by raising the level of achievement from which everyone starts off.

The purpose of equality, then, is to promote difference. The purpose of recognizing and allowing for the indeterminacy of ultimate commitments is to permit unequal persons to share equally in their common culture. The purpose of education is to raise the threshold of personal ability to make power and intellectualism flow together. Finally, the sense in trying to make us more alike in the growing profundity of our uniqueness is to build a personal-social body always better able to take care of itself, our world, and the heritage we shall leave for our followers.

That modernized statement of Adam Smith's Doctrine of the Invisible Hand has, sadly, long since passed out of fashion. By giving up the labor theory of value we drove a wedge between what a man does and control over what he produces. By promoting class and race divisions, we separated men from their total cultures. By divorcing citizenship from meaningful participation, we made of democracy a debating club and a politics which could express itself only in extremes. In sum, by separating our minds from our ability to act, we have turned democracy into a shambles and become collectively stupid. The crisis of our times is not the concatenation of crises—of the simultaneity of stresses in population, urbanization, waste, pollution, and what have you. Rather, the crisis is that we have lost control. Our legally and ideologically posited systems of accountability are either totally gone or severely weakened, for our public institutions have changed in their nature while our underlying ability to think and act upon our thinking has been destroyed by the separation between private thoughts and public acts. It sometimes seems that those who can think cannot act, and those who can act cannot think. No other result should be expected by a people who imagine that action is synonymous with practicality, pragmatism with opportunism, thought with daydreaming, and that the defense of private interests automatically serves the public weal.

The time has arrived in the United States for a grand debate over whether we wish to reconstitute democracy or continue our submersion in elitist authoritarianism. Let us debate honestly, with crystalline frankness, putting aside lies and euphemisms. If the new authoritarians believe that the "masses" are fatally and permanently flawed, untrustworthy, and unworthy of effective or positive political activity in an increasingly specialized and scientific world, then they should say so. Let them put aside the word "democracy" entirely, and explain how they propose to establish sensible governance. If democrats are to make their case, they must rise above propaganda and sentiment and the Cold War, and learn even to transcend the Enlightenment— but not forget it. That is, they must face up to democratic imperatives: Equality must be the precondition for full human attainment however unequal; the link must be broken between inherited private privilege and public advantage; intellectualism must be understood as a skill all may learn, not just a small intelligentsia; and reason and power must flow together in order to create democratic efficacy. The democrat must be willing to give up cowardice, and recognize that a democratic renewal can be brought about only by a mix of reform and structural change. The authoritarian needs to give up ignorance of himself and his premises, own up to his world view and his theory of social causality, and positively state how he thinks his authoritarianism will manage to remain reasonable through time.

But the anti-democrats can do their own talking. In stating the case for the practical need for democracy, the first task is to establish an understanding that our contemporary crisis was made *possible* by the victories of our past democracy, but immediately *caused* by an abandonment of the democratic task. Our cessions of freedom, our failures to practice democracy, our self-abandonment to unreason are the causes of our difficulties. Indeed, we are left with but the shreds of a formal democratic structure. We have still a vast reservoir of informal democracy, though—a generally educated people who are more and more able to deny the legitimacy of undemocratic institutions; communications which inform and sensitize, even though that may not be their intention; a still strong and vital democratic tradition; and a legal system built to permit completion of the democratic promise. The disjunction between intellectualism and power is given form in the disjunction between this informal polity and our formal structures. Similarly, we are still a most powerful democratic *nation*, although we play host to an ever-weakening authoritarian *state*.

The more usual way to express this situation is to say that we have lost our system of social accountability, the structure which Locke and Montesquieu had sought and which our political constitution describes, whose prime purpose is to control tyrants and provide the means of self-control to free men. But this argument can be advanced only by addressing ourselves to the specific circumstances of our present situation, circumstances which reveal in case after case that anti-democracy has brought weakness and irrationality instead of strength and reason.

The low ebb which we have now reached in terms of public confidence in our political institutions and leadership reflects the historic failure of a form of political rule which emerged from World War II and reached its maturity during the various administrations of the sixties. For the first time in its history America was not only ruled by elites, but elitism itself was openly proclaimed and elaborately legitimated. . . .

What is important is that elitism has not only failed but failed spectacularly. Those who controlled this country had at their disposal the most awesome political, military, technological, economic, and scientific system ever assembled. Now much of it is a shambles. An elite which squandered power so prodigally must surely put to shame the most extravagant proponent of egalitarian social policies.[2]

We will have to pick through the rubble willed us by our elitist managers to gain an idea of the magnitude of the task of reconstructing control facing us.

Nuclear Energy We may as well start with the atom and its products, for carelessness here threatens physical survival, whether through formal warfare among superpowers, the activities of terrorists, the disposition of nuclear wastes, the explosion of power plants, or even the desperation of a small nuclear power *in extremis,* as in the Middle East. Certainly it is disquieting that a few men in Washington and Moscow have control of bombs, rockets, and guidance systems sufficient to destroy the world many times over. The reason for entrusting the use of these weapons to a few men is clear. Response to or initiation of a nuclear attack must be secret and rapid. There is simply no time for the pursuit of a complex and constitutional process under such conditions.

The horror of nuclear warfare has inhibited world wars, of course, but it has also poisoned the international atmosphere with the cruelties of unconventional warfare and has legitimized war among surrogates of the big powers. The effect of seeking to fight "limited wars" is that the United States and other powerful nations have found themselves embroiled in what are actually revolutions and civil wars. We legitimated such interference with the "doctrine of internal warfare," espousing the idea that the Communist enemy would seek to gain victories through civil violence and that an adequate response required our intervention, with appropriate changes in tactics—use of the Green Berets, Vietnam's Operation Phoenix that destroyed potential and actual civilian sympathizers of the Vietcong, or the "destabilization" and assassination attempts of the Central Intelligence Agency. Formal war could not be declared in Vietnam, for that would have triggered treaty commitments on both sides that would have led to confrontation among the nuclear powers. And murder plots, bribery, and revolutionary activities cannot be discussed in Congress for the obvious reason that such activities are unlawful, and presumably a legislature is committed to the creation of law. In short, the avoidance of nuclear danger has turned both the United States and the Soviet Union into international rogues; made a shambles of international law; perverted our constitutional requirements for the conduct of international relations, the declaration of war, and the appropriations necessary to conduct such activities; and eventually threatened even democracy itself, as our government has forced itself into ever more dishonest tangles in order to proceed with the "protection" of the "national security" and the avoidance of an ultimate showdown.

Escaping the nuclear holocaust has exacted a high price; obviously, falling into it would have been even dearer. But it is evident that the present situation remains very dangerous, and it is also clear that our lives and fortunes are not totally in our own hands, but are, in part, at the mercy of military men and politicians in foreign countries. The only sensible long-range course is one that will gradually lead to a total ban on atomic weaponry of all sorts. Since our now conventional "unconventional warfare" depends upon the existence of atomic weaponry, a total restructuring of international coercive relations are an intrinsic part of atomic disarmament. This reordering must be a long and intricate process, demanding great skill and intelligence, as well as the understanding, forbearance, and collective power of the entire nation. But the logic of atomic power and our government's lack of respect for the domestic sources of its own effectiveness have combined to weaken the very institutions which we are ostensibly defending; they must be strengthened if we are to get out of the present international impasse. Sheldon Wolin has expressed the dilemma most vividly:

The harsh fact is that, at present, conduct of American foreign policy and military planning is premised upon the power of the very institutions which stifle the possibilities within our society . . . Consequently, there is a cruel task awaiting the true politician: he must defend a weakened society in a dangerous world while attempting to encourage a transfer of human capacities from the old set of social forms to the newer ones.[3]

The way out can be found only at home. Disarmament should not first be discussed with the Russians. International monetary agreements should not first be talked over in Paris. Middle Eastern deals should not first be struck on airplanes shuttling among hostile capitals. The place to begin is at home, and the way to begin is by laying out the situation, proposing alternative diagnoses, and eschewing the routine dishonesty of our militarized politicians and our politicized armed forces. We are weakened in our foreign relations for two reasons: American citizens no longer trust in the good sense of their political leaders, and foreigners no longer see moral authority emanating from us, not even the consistency of behavior which might be expected from a clear ethical commitment. A good way to begin rebuilding American power in foreign affairs is by the leaders of this country making a formal promise to the American citizenry to renew respect for international law and treaty commitments, and by insisting in international forums that other countries do the same. They may miss the excitement of planning subversions and invasions, the pleasure in being the invisible hand that moves the fate of nations, but grown men should put away childish delights. The neighbors are on to the game, and the rest of the family is weary of replacing the broken crockery and fixing up the gouged walls and torn sofas.

The Economy The power and glory of the American economic system are not to be denied. Call it what you will—capitalism, monopoly capitalism, late capitalism, people's capitalism, welfare capitalism, a mixed economy—the constant, persistent ability to be ever more productive has with few interruptions characterized the United States since the end of the Civil War. We are often told that Americans, six percent of the world's population, consume half the world's supply of this raw material, two thirds of another, and so forth. Certainly ours is a profligate economy, producing and selling much that we don't "need" but want or are taught to want. Yet leaving this genuine truth aside for the moment, the *organization* of the American economy for *production,* whether of depilatories or of wheat, works in wondrous fashion. Indeed, with the emergence of the multi-national corporation, the transnational corporation, or whatever name one may wish to put to it, we may say that American organizational genius in economic affairs is becoming worldwide.

Therein lies its internal logic and its ultimate threat to American democracy—a threat long latent and sometimes active, but now a matter of utmost concern.

The social costs of the American economy are also high, and becoming higher. For all that we produce and consume, too many of us are poor in goods and services, too many of us are ill, unemployed, uncertain, and deprived of pride, bored in routine occupations, and rendered incapable of managing our personal affairs by factors beyond our control and, often, our comprehension. Inflation is a theft of money, pollution a theft of health, monopoly a theft of quality as well as coin, and bribery a theft of pride and power. These defects of our economic life threaten democracy. By the exclusion of large groups from consistent and sensible economic activity, and by the creation of material insecurities among many more, the economy conduces both to lessening the number of real citizens and to creating at least faddish and at worst psychotic political tempers.

The stress between the American economic system and democratic process reflects a stress within the economy itself: The success of a corporate particle no longer can be confidently expected to add to the success of economic performance as a whole. The rational acquisitiveness of one company, in other words, may lead to prosperity for that single organization but may reduce the success, or profitability, of the whole. Joy for the purveyors of oil spells unemployment for automobile workers and distress for automobile manufacturers. Cheap labor in the South pulls textile plants out of New England cities, helps to start a process involving migration from the Caribbean and other methods to cheapen the price of labor still further, affects the cities' tax bases, and eventuates in a massive loss in value of the social and private capital of urban areas. In a prescient article written in the 1930s, Werner Sombart pointed out the strain between the benefit of the few and the loss of all:

While individual action under capitalism is informed by the ideal of highest rationality, the capitalistic system as a whole remains irrational, because the other dominant capitalistic idea, that of acquisition, of the unrestricted assertion by the individual of his power, leaves the regulation of the total economic process to the uncoordinated discretion of individual economic agents. From this coexistence of well nigh perfect rationality and of the greatest irrationality originate the numerous strains and stresses which are peculiarly characteristic of the economic system of capitalism.[4]

Unfortunately, in recent years even the "well nigh perfect rationality" of the individual company has been suffering. The bureaucratic rationalization of business, its "managerialization," helps to stabilize it but reduces its daring, innovation, and gambling spirit. Businessmen, being no more reluctant to seek security than anybody else, eschew the risks of the marketplace and seek the comfort of total monopoly, or shared monopoly, within a framework of technically defined knowledge they can call their own. Sombart finished his classic article with the comment, " 'Stabilization of business' seems to be both the slogan and the accomplishment of this period." [5] This routinization, however, responds to the *government's* attempts to reduce the social costs of business fluctuation, not only the desires of managers themselves. Government regulation of *all* business (not only public-utility monopolies), government-owned business, social security legislation, trade union activities, the government's attempts at countercyclical interventions in the economy, "fine-tuning" and the rest of the structure of welfare-capitalism—these have created a political economy which is more bureaucratized, less subject to market controls in any refined way, and engaged in a kind of technocratic planning that is unable to accommodate the good of the unit with the benefit of the whole. Some of the trite ways in which we have distinguished socialist from capitalist economies are, then, no longer true.

The organization of modern capitalistic business corporations has come to resemble that of governmental corporations and bureaus. There are also obvious similarities in organization and operation between a Soviet trust and a large capitalistic corporation, just as there are similarities between governmental bureaus or public corporations, such as the Tennessee Valley Authority . . . and private corporations, such as the United States Steel Corporation. . . .[6]

Obviously, the "new class" of the socialist countries and capitalist managers share much in style, way of thought, and daily activities. Both groups must relate their activities to the state, they have high social status, and they share the same technocratic ideology that underlies precisely the same technical processes, such as linear economic programming. There are obvious differences of great moment, however. Socialists think of polity and economy as indivisible. And much of what we in the United States call "economic activity" is, in socialist countries, part of the social-support system—education, medicine, vacations and many other privileges, licences to buy what are considered luxury consumer items, and so forth. And labor in socialist societies is in effect assigned to occupations, through a complex process of selection and self-selection. The contemporary capitalist tries to draw a much sharper distinction between economic and political realms, despite the political-economic tradition in capitalism. Market symbols mediate all, including basic social services. And businessmen and capitalist managers must contend with a complex labor force, partly presenting itself on an entirely individualistic basis, partly involved in collective bargaining, and sometimes geographically and even socially mobile.

From a democratic viewpoint, however, neither mode of production is any longer conducive to a free society. Even though socialists seriously attempt to provide basic goods and services equally to all, that in itself has obviously not produced societies with equality before the laws, freedom from unreasonable search and seizure, from police brutality, from extreme repression for political dissidence, or from the other brutish unpleasantnesses of the police state. One might wish to forgive the political sins of the young socialist nations in the Third World, and say that they are still in transition from colonialism, still engaged in rooting out the evils of "bourgeois society." But is the Soviet Union still in transition after more than a half-century of "experimentation"? The common error of both vulgar socialists and vulgar capitalists is that they think politics is a by-product of "materialist" or economic factors. It is historically indisputable that a decent politics is not a necessary effect of any particular economic, or even of any political-economic, system.

The word "capitalism" was invented by early socialist thinkers to define what they detested. The capitalists assumed that social development would flow from the private ability to engage in rational acquisitiveness; democracy could serve and be served by only that way of organizing production. In the long run, the pricing mechanism would distribute equitably to economically active persons what it was they wanted to consume. The socialists, however, assumed that the social good could be wrought only by unalienated labor, out of the joyous and socially constructive work of people in control of the effects of their own actions and the fruits of their own production. In the classical concept of socialism, the production of goods and services would be governed by the political-economic expression of intrinsic human need. Social involvement would enable and lead persons to produce in accordance with ability, and consume in accordance with need. As concepts, socialism and capitalism are exactly contemporaneous. As political-economic systems, they share essentially the same machinery and the same managerial techniques. For whatever reasons of insufficiency of ability or commitment, weakness of ideology, personal attachment to material incentives, or whatever else may be the case, socialist societies have been unable to dispense with the structures of behavior and command that characterize all other industrial societies. And most of them lack the traditions of free labor, contract, and democratic spirit that ameliorate the inherent aristocratic-management tendencies one sees in Western capitalism. The issue of the age, then, is the same for all industrialized societies: it is the question of freedom and its institutionalization, not of socialism versus capitalism as we know each today.

As socialist practice has been unable to bring economic and political equity into a mutually reinforcing relation, American practice and theory have also proven generally unable to accommodate the formally and presumptively separate political and economic institutions in furtherance of the long-term growth of democracy. There are two major schools of orthodox, "capitalistic" economists in the United States. The one that is called "classical," composed of proponents of "micro-economics" and sometimes sneeringly referred to as "the Chicago Boys," argues that private motivation, rationalism, and the free market (that is, a market uncontrolled except by actors moved by the profit motive) remain viable concepts as well as practices, and are the best guides to the creation of wealth. They assume that a freely self-adjusting economy is possible, although corporate units are enormous in size, and that their prosperity must in the long run trickle down to the less favored. The opposing, neo-Keynesian school of "macro-economists" argues that gigantism, economies of scale, and legitimate public-utility monopolies do not conduce to a rapidly reacting free market. Thus, the kind of competition we have adjusts the economy so grossly and slowly that many millions of persons around the world suffer extreme deprivations in the heavings of even normal economic peristalsis, let alone during cyclical tremors. Worse, a monopolized, gigantized economy gains the power to reduce labor costs through periodic depressions that create pools of unemployment or what the Marxists call a "reserve labor army." Inflation is another device to attain the same end, for weakened unions cannot keep labor costs equal to price-rises, and inflation thus becomes a device for hidden profit-taking. The macro-economic school, then, argues for a mix of governmental and private cooperation and planning, countercyclical governmental interventions in the economy, credit and banking regulations to affect monetary factors, and social insurance schemes to minimize the social effects of under- and unemployment, old age, illness, and the other afflictions most people are economically unable to handle for themselves.

Neither school has helped to give us a socially rational economy—one that uses human talent fully and well, minimizes waste, and takes into account the total social costs of producing and distributing. The micro-economists excuse themselves by saying that no society has been willing to try their radical self-governing egotism. But the answer to that statement is that no society has been willing to undertake radical anarchism, either. Both approaches are romantically puristic; their logic is only formal, neither social nor realistic. The macro-economists argue that our government's policy is schizophrenic—motivated by the utopian mythology of the micro-economists, but impelled by the social reality of distress and of the real interdependence of the political and economic orders. Whatever may be the case, our economic life is far behind its potential on all fronts, even the obvious one of full employment of plant capacity, let alone full employment of the talents of the people. The list of failures is well known: the decay of the rail system, the loss of farmland to highways and urban sprawl, the destruction of once productive and gratifying urban neighborhoods, the devastation of aesthetic values, the persistence of underclasses, the sadness of the work life of so many.

These patent failures have caused ideological and political confusion and a wholesale blame-casting that does not clarify the issues. Perhaps the root cause of the general failure to understand the economic crisis lies in that very term; in the early days of the Republic, the crisis would have been seen as a *political-economic* crisis, and thus rooted in questions of ethical preferences and understandings. A "proper" economics in that view was not merely one productive of material goods; it was one that satisfied ethical norms, that was in consonance with "nature." The purpose of production was the satisfaction of political and thus ethical as well as of material wants. Therefore, the *way* of producing was a good in itself, and the *fact* of production was an instrumental consequence to be turned to the satisfaction of other, more substantive expressive needs. But both our orthodox schools of economics have abandoned a direct involvement with the ethics of political economics. Therefore, neither has anything more direct to say about democracy than does the socialist economic planner.

If we are to return to thinking about the relations between economic activity and democratic activity, then we must return to political thought, long since abandoned by the economists of capitalistic systems. The intellectual requirements even of primitive capitalism, dating back to the city-states of the late medieval period, are subtle, and they remain of intrinsic import to the later development of democratic thought. Money needed to be universally accepted, worth needed to be removed from sacred ascription alone, personal talent needed to be recognized in the here and now, and contract needed to be respected in order to reward the merit of any worthy actor as well as to infuse the "system" with consistency and thus predictability through time. Machiavelli, the great political theoretician of the time, drove the necessarily secular characteristics of early capitalism to their political and social outer limits. The establishment and maintenance of secular power was his subject, and he brooked no mystifications as he lay down the case for the consensual creation of power the intelligent prince would seek, or the knavery the not-so-intelligent prince would employ to keep that one "commodity"—power—which gives reality to whatever men may think or desire.

"Developmental" capitalism, that flourishing of productive ability which started in England slowly in the seventeenth century and spread more and more rapidly with the growth of formal democracy, justified itself on more "religious" bases than the bold laicism of Machiavelli. The reintroduction of natural law, in Protestant form, by Hobbes, Locke, and many others established an assumed ethical basis for proper institutional conduct. We see the results in our Constitution. In economic affairs democracy gave an enormous push to what Machiavelli and other thinkers of his time had begun to justify. Impersonal and trusting social cooperation needed for the creation of a citizenry also enlarges the work force, the number of consumers, and the number of persons who can think contractually and, thus, in the future-oriented perspective required by round-about and specialized production. When the divide between the aristocracy and the bourgeoisie was crossed, the social as well as economic fruits of development were enlarged, and this in turn extended educational systems to be ratified and broadened the recruitment base for new entrepreneurs. When the bonds first of serfdom and then of slavery were dissolved, labor became physically free and occupationally mobile. Its cheapness was guaranteed for a long time by imposing the myth that the seller of labor was legally and thus contractually equal to the buyer of labor. (Machiavelli's understanding of the nature of power was swept under the rug. The lump is still there, however.)

As capitalistic economies bloomed, the capitalistic countries became metropoles and expanded into colonial empires. Even the poor people in the mother countries then began to be able to enjoy "surplus-value," the product of labor even cheaper than their own. This relaxation of pressure on the lower groups in industrializing societies encouraged a slow but steady expansion of meaningful citizenship—in other words, of a structured, formal ability to exercise power. The political structures of the new capitalistic societies could, then, begin to speak meaningfully in terms of most persons within their borders; they could become reasonably complete nation-states. Something akin to a national interest shared by all could be and, indeed, often was meaningfully spoken of. The rapid increase in wealth and the expansion of significant power, sometimes fueled by blood, gave hope even to those outside the effective polity that they might eventually be incorporated. But only in a very few lands was the job of building citizenship completed. The Scandinavian countries, the Netherlands, and to a lesser extent Switzerland are those exemplars. No other countries have as yet managed to complete the construction of a universal national citizenry. A major reason for the incompleteness of the political mandate of the French and American Revolutions must be traced back to the beginning of the period of "mature" capitalism, usually dated as occurring after World War I. It was then that the growth of capitalism into gigantism and monopoly began to impede the growth of democracy and, in many lands, become entirely antithetical to it. Nazi Germany is, of course, the most painful example of the incompatibility between monopolized, private economies and public democracy.

The first step in rethinking political and economic relations is to fuse them at base with a common ethic. This classical device will permit us to think of a "political-economy" not as a politicized economy, or as an economically corrupted polity, but as a compound of varied functions held together, or "politicized," by a common set of values, both instrumental and ultimate. A democratic political-economy must begin and end with the person-in-society, seeing him as both end and means, and combining his reason and his actions in his empowered participation. Only a return to the ethic of the labor theory of value can reconcile economics and politics within the same grand political frame. Perhaps economists will have trouble measuring the relation between labor-value and market-price. They will be unable to do so if they continue to exclude the idea of power as part of any price. In the meantime, let the rest of us return to using pricing as the lens through which we see the effective demand of value-producing people. And let the rest of us, too, begin to understand that all capital investment is only in persons— their ability to live and work together in social comity, their ability to create as well as produce. Therefore, a democratic political economy must assume as its elemental "capital-producing" task the building of a common floor of political, economic, and social abilities under all competent citizens. Appropriate educational levels provided to healthy people assured of the opportunity to work are the primary conditions for establishing the equality of economic condition upon which secondary differences according to skills and ambitions may be mounted.

A political economy is more, of course, than a mass of trained, interacting, loyal, and interested citizens. It is also a complex of specialized functions and structures which demand appropriate systems of accountability. Even a strong, informed, and active body politic can be confounded by interlocking directorates of bureaucrats engaged in furious self-protection. Even a university-bred lawyer can pass bribes, bend regulatory agencies to business advantage, or use business advantage to certify his prestige with a political appointment. No perfect solution to these tugs-and-pulls will be found, but awareness of the ethical point from which democratic economic and political activities depart, and conscious attention to the fact that continued and effective political action is also economically meaningful can keep threats to the democratic order in check.

The general political-economic order can be policed only as I have just said: by the constant attention of organized citizens. But we may also be arriving at the stage in which the dream of the laissez-faire micro-economists can be made partially true; that is, we may be coming to a situation in which personal enlightenment is so reinforced with advanced technology that the pursuit of private advantage can be made to serve the social good through a self-correcting marketplace dealing in secondary goods and services. As I have already said, modern technology now makes efficiency possible in relatively small operations in many fields of manufactures. Flexibility in plant location also makes centralization and decentralization mutually compatible. But let us not forget that a meaningfully free market depends upon a substantively free citizenry. And such a citizenry, in turn, needs an economy which gives them that basis of intellectual and economic power which is the precondition for a truly "capitalistic" market. We shall not achieve an abundance of the universally needed until we unleash the total productive capacity of the nation. To do so, we must stop thinking of persons as "superfluous" or thinking of the "population problem" as the origin of poverty. Poverty results from the nonuse or misuse of people in creating wealth; poverty is the product of organizational defects which impede people from creating wealth.

We shall require structural changes in our economy and the revival and reformulation of the mother-ideas of our culture before we can reconstruct a democratic political economy. The master problem is not economic. It is *political*-economic. That understanding is the first step toward expressing a problem whose solution is a democratic necessity.

La trahison des elites A distressing and profound problem in American life is the inability of many parts of our elite to decide on their "constituency," to determine where their ultimate loyalty lies. Much of the widespread suspicion of our foreign-aid programs, the conduct of our foreign policy, and big business is a reaction to the ambivalence affecting almost all elite groups, not merely those in political, military, or business affairs. The conflict of loyalties involves ideological as well as easily understandable material interests. Consequently, the national interest has become almost impossible to define, for the interests of elites are not the same as those of the entire society. Just as we are locked in a sterile argument about centralization and decentralization in our domestic political organization, as though the two forms were not mutually compatible, in foreign affairs our elites have proceeded as though broadening and deepening our national political community were necessarily antithetical to international comity. This false intellectual construction of the case, pointed out in Chapter 3, is sadly descriptive of the real situation: The treason of the elites has, indeed, created a contradiction between our national power and the continued satisfaction of special interest abroad.

The persons partly responsible for pushing America's inflation, for twisting foreign policy through bribes and conniving with foreign cartels, for overthrowing foreign governments, and for soliciting foreign moral and financial support for American elections do not see themselves as disloyal to their fellow citizens or destructive of the American system of governance. Business executives argue that their subornations contribute to American prosperity. Saboteurs and *agents provocateurs* say they are buttressing our ideological health and security. Oil company executives argue that high prices and working capital will make America independent of foreign sources of energy. Politicians, publicists, and others who accept foreign funds to affect domestic American politics try to keep quiet about it, but still excuse themselves on the grounds that America, after all, is a world power and thus has a global constituency which is affected when substantive changes in our society occur; therefore foreigners should have some "representation" in the determination of domestic decisions. The assumption lying behind all these agruments is, again, the old and thoroughly discredited "trickle-theory," that what is good for the people on top will drip down to the less fortunate below. Of course, the very reliance on foreign constituencies strengthens those who have them, and weakens those who do not, thus reinforcing the already formidable dike between the "ins" and "outs" which prevents the trickle. Obviously, the entire process also removes an increasingly important part of political and economic life from the scope of the laws, opening another way to escape accountability.

The American public has been asked only to ratify the major international events which were engineered over the past fifteen years by the political and economic elites of the United States. The cartels and multi-national corporations have worked their inflationary and recessionary way with virtual impunity, while the government has repeatedly demonstrated its greater loyalty to allies abroad than to citizens at home who may disagree with its actions. American political leaders pursued in word and deed an almost unlimited commitment to corrupt South Vietnamese allies; simultaneously, they maintained in word and deed an almost unlimited enmity to fellow Americans who exercised the democratic duty of disagreement. Those youngsters who protested with their feet are condemned to exile; those Americans who disagreed with their mouths were put on black lists, denied political appointment, harassed by the

Internal Revenue Service, and otherwise informed that their state considered them undesirables.

The pretense that such shameful behavior is in the interest of us all leads to an even more basic violation of democratic principle—persistent lying, which renders impossible rational and reasonable judgments about the course of the state. The "secret" war in Cambodia was a secret only to Americans, for example. Certainly the Cambodians and Vietnamese knew all about it, as did any reader of *Le Monde*. Who it was that "destabilized" Guatemala, the Dominican Republic, Chile, Iran, and many other nations was at the time well known to the foreigners concerned, while for Americans the activities were state secrets. The menace to American democracy inherent in these practices should not be minimized. The "logic" of extending ideological colleagueship laterally across national boundaries, and denying community loyalty downward to the citizenry allegedly represented, is that one's fellow citizens became the enemy in the event of disagreement. What is more obvious, viewed in that light, than that the American government should seek to "protect" itself against American citizens by importing the tactics it has used overseas—infiltration of "dissident" groups, wiretapping of citizens, physical isolation from the citizenry, elaborate plans for distorting understandings, and the "siege mentality" of recent administrations?

These antinational actions are not restricted to the violent aspects of international relations. They characterize, if more subtly, what may seem to be even enlightened foreign policy. For example, the view that customs unions, free trade associations, and common markets are always desirable is often entirely inconsistent with sound national growth, especially for developing societies. Economic unions seek to enlarge markets and rationalize production by going laterally across national boundaries—from privileged group in one country to privileged group in another country. Again the justification is that the benefits to those on top will find their way to those on the bottom. But again the more direct and truly democratic way is denied. The most efficient way to recruit people for nation-building is to go directly at it, to establish social mechanisms that will permit people to become more productive citizens. Searching for the indirect way is but an exercise in the enlargement of privilege, the increase of distance separating social groups, the denial of nation and with it of democracy.

As in the case of nuclear arms and the economy, submitting our elites to law and to political and economic accountability will be a complex and demanding task. The grounds exist for proceeding with the job, however, even in elite groups themselves. Some elements of the elite have shown themselves to be inexpert as well as disloyal, but other major segments have not been involved in the game. Indeed, great strains are evident between pro- and antinational factions in American leadership. Bankers, industrialists, military men, and politicians divide on that very issue. Its salience needs to be brought to the fore, the mincing of words must be stopped, and what laws exist must be applied. If not, our upper group will continue to tear itself apart—as is evident in the attacks made on the "eastern establishment" by the southwestern and western "establishments," by the acrimonious debate among those who count themselves as conservatives, by the confused relations between trade-union elites and commercial and industrial elites, and by the hollowness and ineffectuality of almost all academic thought on international affairs. In other words, the subject of the loyalty of our elites is already on the agenda, and sides are already drawn. And this issue is one of the few that can be immediately and directly clarified by proper and fitting diagnosis, by posing the issue in stark and realistic terms so that the often unwitting disloyalty of many people can be corrected by themselves, by the voters, and by the courts. Many business and political leaders pride themselves on being hardnosed, realistic, tied to the "facts." Well, gentlemen, and the few ladies among you, obey your own dictum. Your pursuit of your own interests has contradicted the interests of the nation in all too many cases. A lot of us do not like it. Are you truly comfortable with the role you have been playing? Can you adjust your behavior to the democratic rhetoric you have been purveying these many years? Or have you given up the words "free society," just as you have given up "free enterprise" for the at least more accurate "private enterprise"?

Research and Experimentation America's scientific work is out of control in two essential aspects: The production of scientific knowledge is little constrained by professional and scientific ethics, and is more and more funded and shaped in ways inhibiting "basic" research; and the "consumption" of scientific knowledge and technical advance is somewhat misdirected, the possibilities unknown even to potentially knowledgeable consumers. With particular relevance to our subject, it can be said that very little new technology or scientific knowledge has been consciously applied to the problems of democracy itself. On the contrary, scientists have all too often wrapped themselves in the mysteries of their trade and presumed upon their high status, to the detriment of expanded understanding and use of reason. The very style of thought of "hard" scientists—all too often mechanistic and deterministic—buttresses uncontrolled elitism, and applies an incorrect understanding of social life to our problems. Physical and natural scientists tend to think of people as though they were molecules, perfectly distributed in some "flux" or another.

Recent advances in biology, the possibilities of viral mutations, risks associated with nuclear plants, cloning, and many other examples of the continuing vitality of scientific thought raise many ethical questions. One widely debated issue is the question of whose life should be preserved by new, still expensive, and scarce medical techniques. Of greater immediate moment are the risks of irretrievable destruction of environment and life inherent in certain technologies, especially in biological experimentation. Because the risk factor is so high, elaborate safeguards are usually taken, although in industry there are cases where the desire for profit has overridden knowledge of the threats involved. But, by and large, the scientific community tries to establish ironclad protections against loss of control over its experiments and the technological processes gained from some of them. Paradoxically, the lower the probability of loss of control, the higher the cost of such loss. The reason, of course, is that risk always increases the more a total organism is involved. Correlatively, the simpler the organism, the greater the threat to its survival posed by any intervention. That obvious biological statement has a political moral, for the same relation between simplicity and threats to survival holds for societies.

The ethical standards guiding physical, natural, and social scientists are loose, almost entirely without sanction, sometimes irrelevant to changing conditions, and widely varied from discipline to discipline. Worse, the ethical norms guiding the buyers of research have nothing to do with the ethics of science itself. The best known ethical spasm which seized on the scientific community in recent years concerned the atomic bomb and its hydrogen offspring, and came to a head in but did not end with the Oppenheimer case. Less well known, but of equally serious ethical moment, is the relationship of social-science advisers to totalitarian political systems. Some economists, in particular, are prone to lend their services to any government which requests them. To the extent to which economists strengthen such governments, they also destroy the other social sciences within the society affected.

The problem is political as well as ethical, for the sciences cannot operate in the absence of that freedom, self-correction, and relativism which the ongoing practice of democracy demands. This is absolutely true of the social sciences, almost as true for the biological or life sciences, and generally holds even for the physical sciences. As capitalism and democracy developed together, so did science and democracy. And as the economic and political orders have drifted into contradiction, the same may occur between science uncontrolled and the politics of democracy. If so, we shall be left without the intellectualizing influences of social theory and the social sciences, and the natural and physical sciences will degenerate into mere technology. We know full well that science has gained no foothold in any underdeveloped and, thus, authoritarian state. We know, too, that the social sciences died in Nazi Germany and Fascist Italy, and never succeeded in building themselves in corporate Iberia. The humanities and the social sciences in the Soviet Union are at a pitifully low ebb, and the natural and physical sciences—despite the official encouragement and contained freedom given Soviet scientists—tend in many fields to lag behind those of even much smaller Western nations, such as Germany and even France.

Science requires freedom from other than scientific sanction for failure, freedom to define the scientifically significant, freedom within which to establish the methodologically necessary pretense to "objectivity" or "neutrality"—the temporary suspension of values for the purposes of a particular piece of research. But the entire enterprise requires a further, underlying commitment: the relativizing belief in uncertainty that permits premises and hypotheses to remain constant only so long as they are not falsified. It is on that basis that science gains its dynamism, its ability to "push back the frontiers of knowledge," as the hackneyed phrase puts it. It is on that very basis, too, that democracy gains its power to change without breaking. A scientific establishment unaware of the ethical political conditions for its existence is, then, ignorant of the foundations of its own methodology. The public obligation of a science that seeks to maintain its own institutional integrity is the enlargement of democratic capacity. But with respect to the consumption of science and technology for political purposes, our scientific estates have been by and large counted as absent.

Little by way of overt democratic theorizing has come from the social sciences for many generations. Rather, we have been subject to antidemocratic postulations. Similarly, no serious consideration has been given by "hard" scientists to the structure of the social environment needed for their work. Both groups have complained often enough about a lack of support, but neither has gone on to ask general social organizational questions. For example, we have been told a great deal about American elections, but little about how issues might be explicitly defined and voted upon to expand the possibilities inherent in the American situation. Our political studies have been too reactive, and not innovative enough in creating understanding of the varied ways to pose problems. Communications and administrative control through information flows have been designed for many units of government, but almost nothing has been done about the substance of communications, and about synthesizing the analytical materials that flow in those information systems. Instead, the dictum that the medium is the message has reigned, and so the tendency to think of governance as administration-devoid-of-politics has been enhanced.

American scientists produced no major studies of race in American society between about 1950 and the early 1960s. The violence of the 1960s was not predicted, and instead, major American social scientists argued the impossibility of such happenings. Famous scholars were deeply involved in planning and thinking about the Vietnam war, all to no avail. And now that we are beset by crises in the cities, the callous evasion of central governmental responsibility which is involved in the "new federalism," the inability of state and local governments to assume the burdens imposed by Washington's derelictions, and the other difficulties mentioned throughout this book, we have no academic scientific consensus on which to draw. Instead, scholars are as distraught as everyone else, as devoid of paradigms or crystallized understandings to work from.

If scientists had not abandoned the effort to understand the dimensions of their social situation—as presumably they do not neglect the constants in their experimental situations and designs—then we would be politically better off. Scholars are usually blessed with tenure so that they may serve the public need by thinking freshly, openly, creatively, originally, in exploration of the alternatives possible to a society. Why else do we so jealously guard academic freedom? Why is it that we do not equally jealously guard the political freedom providing the guarantee behind academic freedom? Had academics done so, they would have been better scientists as well as better citizens.

The Choice The United States was the first country to establish a state committed to the ideal of ensuring a free people in a free nation. It can also be the first to realize this vision, the first to transcend the limitations of middle-class democracy and achieve a wholeness of the experience of freedom. It can go beyond the antiquated conflicts between socialism and capitalism, and between private good and the public welfare, and so become immune to the appeals of unreason and totalitarianism. It can be the first to escape the fact as well as the premise of everlasting scarcity. It can be the first to blend reason fully into power, giving everyday meaning to the power of reason and to the reasoned use of power. It can complete the sense of its philosophical origins, and thus move past them, subordinating state to nation and permitting an organically whole society of persons to be evermore varied in their personalities and abilities because they evermore commonly share in the creation and uses of their culture.

No great new inventions of thought or machine are needed for this fulfillment of our historical promise. The necessary conditions for it exist; the sufficient ones can be made out of our stock of understandings. That is, the bits and pieces are at hand with which the structure of a total democracy can be made, but the understandings and power needed to put them together have not coalesced. The constituent elements include our classical national tradition, a legal system already partially constituted to permit a free populace to order itself, a literate and broadly though incompletely educated citizenry, a communications net of universal reach, and a long tradition as well as practice of intricately meshed social interaction based on a goodly measure of personal trust and loyalty to the structure of society.

The understanding required to organize those elements into a total democratic conception is that the unity binding all behavior in a free society is—no matter in what diverse spheres—infused with a common ethic. That underlying value takes its political expression in the concept that the way one acts is part of the goal for which one acts. Democratic goals cannot be reached by undemocratic means; such a process betrays its ostensible purpose. Similarly, the use of democratic means for undemocratic ends weakens or destroys both the democratic instrumentalities employed and the undemocratic goals that may be reached. Unity of means and ends is the key element in infusing process itself with moral value, an identification critical to the maintenance of dynamism within continuing freedom. The process is means and end, doing and direction, instrument and satisfaction in itself. Its purpose is to permit control and achievement in a given moment, and in that selfsame moment to allow an expansion of control and achievement for future moments. The political project of freedom, then, is not the "solution" of this or that given "problem." Rather, the politics of democracy concern the procedures that open the flow of minds and power to symbolizing, diagnosing, and resolving problems in social life—"problems" because they threaten to restrict choice to limits narrower than the full sense and effectiveness which a society can bring to bear in its self-governance at any given time.

It follows, then, that the way to begin assuring the choice of democracy for the United States is to begin to live it immediately, in small ways and large, in thought and in action. Civility, generosity, courtesy, and honesty honor the basic premise of democracy—its commitment to uncertainty—and give it life in the most vulgar as well as noble of activities. Civility is respect for the ultimate differences among us. Generosity is the graciousness of giving, and taking. Courtesy is the respect for the integrity of another's *persona,* the guarding of forms which banish indignity. Honesty is the basis for an accurate touching of minds and a sharing of understandings. To those basic decencies one must add courage—the strength to shun dishonesty when custom and authority permit it, to point out incompetence when ideological and group interest promotes it, and to run the risk of error and the humiliation of admitting error when trying to think out more reasonable explanations. These characteristics of democratic temper and behavior are not the pablum of which sententious sermons are made. Their absence in American public life is notorious—and it is in that absence that their importance is most acutely known. But it is in their exercise that the sufficient conditions for completing the democratic project rest.

The problems of democracy cannot be solved by offering concrete solutions. Bussing, pollution, racism, violence, crime, the cities—these are not the problems of democracy. They are the problems created by the lack of democracy. They are specific maladjustments in a society that has not mustered the skill, temper, or power to keep itself together. The problems of democracy, however, concern instead how to permit intelligence and effectiveness to be brought to bear in the reestablishment of self-governance, self-determination, self-adjustment, and self-definition. This problematic is the basic one, and begins to be resolved the moment that we start acting and thinking as self-governing, self-determining, self-adjusting, and self-defining

THE REASON FOR FREEDOM

people. If the ends and means of democracy cannot be separated, then it follows that beginning democratically to solve the problems of democracy also begins to solve *the* problem.

This prescription may appear arch and unrealistic. Confronted with the difficulties of contemporary American life, almost all writers on social themes in this decade have advanced entirely different alternatives. Some reject the machine and the modern estate totally, and seek a return to smallness and even to medievalism. Others dismiss participant democracy totally, as an unattainable dream, and propose the rule of philosopher-kings, engineer-kings, or sociologist-kings. Others support corporate fascism in one or another guise, the organization of persons according to their occupational identifications and the building of community around job-related hierarchy and physical location. Some Marxists argue for a dictatorship of the proletariat in classical Soviet style. Still other writers are nihilists, rejecting all they see and assuming that something better must rise from the shards left by total destruction. All these "solutions" are undesirable, and all but two of them unlikely. The issue is, of course, whether democracy is itself possible.

The two most probable undemocratic outcomes are, generally, of the elitist and corporatist types. In structure our society has already assumed some part of those forms. But this is probably less important than the fact that so many people accept elitist ideologies, and that our present authoritarianism has deepened so much—suggesting yet further coercion, the use of the new instruments of total repression which post–World War II technology allows us. Strong and even absolute coercion will be a necessity, in my view, if authoritarianism is the path we choose. The reason is that democracy is yet alive in the land; it remains a viable alternative, and as such it is the enemy of the elitist and the corporatist, an enemy they have already vested in the persons of students and hippies and opponents of the Vietnam War and other people who ask too much of their government. Many millions of other Americans are fated to become similarly undesirable in the event that we continue to see accountability drain from our political order.

The roots of American democracy lie where they must: in people at large, though too many are escapees from freedom.

But the number of true democrats is probably much larger than our institutional means of expression reveal. Certainly most Americans would like not to have to bus their children to distant schools and also would like to make such a choice in the name of self-determination, not of racism. Almost all would like to have law and order, and still be able to disentangle racism from that basic desire. Most of us would like adequate public and private services, and not have to accept the deprivation of others as an inescapable cost of such services. All of us would like a well-functioning economy that would not exact inhuman costs in unemployment and boredom. Turning our intelligence to re-establishing control over our lives, so that legitimate desires are not host to smuggled hatred and unreason, is the job to which our political and intellectual leaders should be addressing them-selves. That most of them instead stoke the fires of irrationalism and confusion is apparent. Can it be that fewer and fewer regis-tered voters are willing to go to the polls because they do not want to make unreasoning and hence undemocratic choices? Can it be that our "elites" cannot or will not hear what a latently democratic people is trying to say?

The 1960s were significant precisely because our leaders were forced to change their ways, if not their thinking. The 1970s have witnessed a continuation of the pressure on the state to reform, to become responsive and more honest. But the formal institutions of the polity—the state, the political parties, the pressure groups, local and state governments—have done little to encourage the democratic spirit, little that evidences an ability to respond to the public's significant and even powerful nay-saying. "Don't Tread on Me" has again become a significant warning in American politics, but this rejection *as affirmation* or something desired—a resumption of reasoned control over our national and personal destinies—falls on deaf ears and pos-sibly dumb minds. Our leaders and our institutions certainly do not make the practice of democracy easy for us.

If democracy is our choice, then the only direction is toward it, and the only way is freely—building organized power through new and established institutions, and making a con-scious attempt to think our way through the situation. We prob-ably need less of the power component in democracy than we do of the knowledge factor, for we are still in many significant ways a free society, an exciting and open one. What we lack, by and large, is the habit of thinking about action in a democratic manner. Conceptualization, intellectualization, debate, honest grappling—these we need, before we lose what ability we still have to translate our ideas into the power to control ourselves as well as those who are increasing their control over us.

To this idea I have dedicated this book.

NOTES

Chapter 1   CHOOSING SIDES

1. "Introduction," *The Federalist Papers* (1961), pp. xiv–xv.

2. *The Origins of American Politics* (1970), p. 56.

3. Ernst Cassirer, *The Myth of the State* (1946), p. 76.

4. As quoted in Ernst Cassirer, *The Philosophy of the Enlightenment* (1951), p. 212.

5. As quoted in Ernst Cassirer, *Rousseau, Kant, and Goethe* (1970), p. 26. Originally from *Rousseau, Judge of Jean-Jacques.*

6. Ernst Cassirer, *The Philosophy of the Enlightenment*, pp. 13–14.

7. As quoted in Ernst Cassirer, *The Myth of the State*, p. 153.

Chapter 2   THE AMERICAN REVOLUTIONARY ETHIC AND ITS BETRAYAL

1. Henry Steele Commager, *The Development of a Revolutionary Mentality* (1972), p. 7.

2. Charles A. Beard, *An Economic Interpretation of the Constitution of the United States* (1965), p. 188.

3. *Science and Sentiment in America* (1972), p. 10.

4. John Locke, *Two Treatises of Civil Government* (1924), p. 143.

5. For an exhaustive discussion of these issues, see Joseph Tussman and Jacobus tenBroek, "The Equal Protection of the Laws," *California Law Review,* Vol. 37, No. 3, September 1949. Also, Frank L. Michelman, "The Supreme Court 1968 Term. Forward: On Protecting the Poor Through the Fourteenth Amendment," *Harvard Law Review,* Vol. 83, No. 7, May 1970.

6. *The Structure of Freedom* (1968), pp. 36–37.

7. As quoted in James Stevenson, "Senator from Massachusetts," *The New Yorker,* August 25, 1975, p. 75.

8. As quoted in Ernst Cassirer, *The Philosophy of Englightenment* (1951), p. 260.

9. Shlomo Avineri, *The Social and Political Thought of Karl Marx* (1968), p. 44.

10. As quoted in *Ibid.,* pp. 44–45.

11. Coppage *v.* Kansas, 236 U.S. 1, 35 S. Ct. 240, 59L. Ed. 441.

12. Ernst Cassirer, *The Question of Jean-Jacques Rousseau* (1963), p. 55.

13. *Op. cit.,* p. 59.

Chapter 3   THE LONE EAGLE ABROAD

1. This section is in part based on an article entitled "The Kitsch in Hemispheric Realpolitik," which appeared originally, under my authorship, as Chapter 2 of Ronald Hellman and H. Jon Rosenbaum, eds., *Latin America: The Search for a New International Role* (1975), pp. 27–38.

2. *A History of Western Philosophy* (1945), p. 494.

3. Parts of this discussion of Cuba have been abstracted from a piece by my wife, Frieda M. Silvert, and me, entitled "Fate, Chance, and Faith," written after we visited Cuba for several weeks during the summer of 1974 and published by the American Universities Field Staff in September 1974.

4. Osvaldo Sunkel, "Change and Frustration in Chile," in Claudio Véliz, ed., *Obstacles to Change in Latin America* (1965), pp. 134–35.

5. For these and other figures see Markos Mamalakis and Clark Reynolds, *Essays on the Chilean Economy* (1965), p. 146.

6. *Chile: An Amnesty International Report* (1974), p. 9.

7. *Covert Action in Chile 1963–1973*, Staff Report of the Select Committee to Study Governmental Operations with respect to Intelligence Activities, U.S. Senate (1975), pp. 27–28.

8. As cited in *Covert Action in Chile 1963–1973, op cit.*, p. 27.

Chapter 4   THE ETHIC: DENIAL AND AFFIRMATION

1. From "Technology and Social Relations," *New Left Review*, Sept.–Oct. 1966, p. 30.

2. Samuel C. Florman, "In Praise of Technology," *Harper's*, Nov. 1975, p. 54.

3. *Ibid.*, p. 72.

4. "The Human Prospect," *The New York Review of Books*, Jan. 24, 1974, p. 21.

5. Edward C. Banfield and James Q. Wilson, *City Politics* (1963), pp. 3–4.

6. "The United States," in Michael J. Crozier, Samuel P. Huntington, and Joji Watanuki, *The Crisis of Democracy: Report on the Governability of Democracies to the Trilateral Commission* (1975), pp. 59–118.

7. *Ibid.*, pp. 59–60.

8. *Ibid.*, p. 64.

9. Both quotations from *Ibid.*, pp. 114–15.

10. See especially Martin Diamond's elegant article, "The Declaration and the Constitution: Liberty, Democracy, and the Founder," *The Public Interest*, Fall 1975, pp. 39–55. An abridged version of the Huntington piece I have been citing appears in the same issue, which should be read in its entirety as the best single refutation by this school of thought to my own ideas.

11. *Op. cit.*, pp. 6–7.

12. David M. Muchnick, "Death Warrant for the Cities: The National Urban Policy," *Dissent*, Winter, 1975, p. 32.

13. Daniel Bell, "Notes on Post-Industrial Society, I and II," *The Public Interest*, Winter, 1967, p. 29.

14. This argument is exquisitely spelled out in Marlis Krueger and Frieda Silvert, *Dissent Denied: The Technocratic Response to Protest* (1975), pp. 57–61.

15. In "The Politics of Academia," as quoted in Krueger and Silvert, *Ibid.*, pp. 59–60.

16. The bluntest statement I have read of this alleged dilemma is in Michael Crozier's article on Europe in the Report of the Trilateral Commission, as cited, pp. 30–33.

17. Robert Sherrill, reviewing Jonathan Schell's *The Time of Illusion* in *The New York Times Book Review,* Jan. 18, 1976, p. 2.

18. W. Lloyd Warner, Robert J. Havighurst, and Martin R. Loeb, *Who Shall Be Educated? The Challenge of Unequal Opportunities* (1946), p. 56.

19. Frederick Mosteller and Daniel P. Moynihan, "A Pathbreaking Report," in Mosteller and Moynihan, eds., *On Equality of Educational Opportunity* (1972), p. 27.

20. Christopher Jencks, *et al., Inequality: A Reassessment of the Family and Schooling in America* (1973), p. 253.

21. For such a study done on a large scale, see Kalman H. Silvert and Leonard Reissman, *Educational, Class, and Nation: The Educational Experiences of Chile and Venezuela* (1976).

22. T. W. Adorno, Else Frenkel-Brunswick, Daniel J. Levinson, and R. Nevitt Sanford, *The Authoritarian Personality* (1950).

Chapter 5   THE REASON FOR FREEDOM

1. Krueger and Silvert, *op. cit.,* pp. 14–15.

2. Sheldon S. Wolin, "The New Conservatives," *The New York Review of Books,* Feb. 5, 1976, p. 10.

3. *Ibid.,* p. 11.

4. "Capitalism," *Encyclopaedia of the Social Sciences* (1930), Volume No. 3/4, p. 198.

5. *Ibid.,* p. 208.

6. Calvin B. Hoover, "Capitalism," *International Encyclopaedia of the Social Sciences* (1968), Volume II, p. 299.